# Global Hunger:

# A Look at the Problem and Potential Solutions

Malcolm H. Forbes        Lois J. Merrill

Co-Editors

University of Evansville Press 1986

Soc
HD
9018
D44
G57
1986

This series of lectures funded by a grant from
Bristol-Myers Company

ISBN 0-930982-08-8

# TABLE OF CONTENTS

# ACKNOWLEDGEMENT

The University of Evansville is pleased to present this collection of monographs on global hunger in the modern world. These monographs are based upon a series of lectures delivered during 1985 by experts on the subject of human hunger and its diverse and powerful impact upon the political, economic, social, and biological stability of a small and interdependent world of peoples. Individually and collectively, these lectures add significantly to our knowledge and understanding of an immense problem which is both ancient and contemporary. They also present some hopeful directions for the amelioration and eventual eradication of this great scourge.

The University of Evansville is grateful for the generous grant by Bristol-Myers Company which made possible these lectures and their publication. The University also appreciates greatly the co-sponsorship of Mead Johnson and Company, an important part of the Bristol-Myers organization and a renowned research and manufacturing institution in the nutrition and pharmaceutical fields. This collection is dedicated to all the people of the world who are giving their hearts and minds to the conquest of human malnutrition.

Wallace B. Graves
President
University of Evansville

# PREFACE

The call to improve the welfare of deprived persons and populations remains a moral and ethical imperative. Yet, new political and economic realities make it clear that governmental actions alone can not resolve perplexing human problems such as global hunger. Previously uninvolved institutions must become active and new alliances must be formed, if a more satisfactory rate of progress in the war against human suffering is to be achieved. Encouragingly, new segments of our society are becoming concerned and involved, and new coalitions are forming. The six-part lecture series at the University of Evansville and these published proceedings provide evidence of such emerging partnerships.

Sponsorhip by the University of Evansville School of Nursing and Health Sciences with financial support from the Bristol-Myers Company marks a cooperative venture for academia and industry as an alternative to a government-sponsored study or conference. The content of the lectures and these written articles spans the gamut of disciplines as well as approaches that can impact global hunger—science and education, government programs and policies, relief programs and long-term policies. There is now evidence of a broadened perspective being brought to bear on this persistent problem. Involving students and an increasingly concerned public in personal contact with expert lecturers, but expanding the impact of their knowledge via distribution of these printed proceedings, comprise further broadening of the attack on world hunger.

It is particularly appropriate that this lecture series was sponsored by Mead Johnson and Company and its parent company Bristol-Myers. These companies have a long history of involvement in nutrition research and of meeting nutrition-related needs. As the importance of nutrition was recognized both in this country and internationally, the Bristol-Myers Company began a grants program for focussing on nutrition issues. To date the program has provided more than two and one half million dollars in unrestricted grants to thirteen research institutions throughout North America, Europe and Asia for use by investigators who are searching for solutions to problems of nutrition and world hunger.

In addition to the research grants program, Bristol-Myers has also provided for the past four years an individual award for distinguished achievement in nutrition research. One of the larger prizes in this field, it shows the company's commitment to encouraging and supporting excellence. It is my pleasure to be part of an organization which recognizes our responsibility to participate in education and research. I am also delighted to be associated with the University of Evansville which has taken seriously the problem of finding answers to world-wide hunger and malnutrition. We all hope genuinely that the lecture series and the papers published herewith will enhance our individual and collective efforts to overcome the human suffering which hunger creates.

On behalf of Bristol–Myers and the reader of these proceedings, I express my sincerest thanks to the University of Evansville and its School of Nursing and Health Sciences for arranging a panel of world-renowned lecturers who have made presentations of such uniformly high quality.

Wayne A. Davidson, President
U.S. Pharmaceutical and
    Nutritional Group
Bristol–Myers Company

# INTRODUCTION

The topic of global hunger is not an easy one to address, but the speakers in the Bristol-Myers Lecture Series at the University of Evansville have attempted to put the problem in perspective. Each author brings his or her own background and experience to focus on hunger. They all are uniquely qualified to share their understanding with the general public. From the political to the economic, from the philosophical to the practical, from the physiological to the emotional, from the success to the suffering—all these factores are taken into consideration.

The individuals who have provided manuscripts for this volume were chosen because of their involvement or interest in the study of hunger throughout the world. While their viewpoints differ, they join in the universal concern for people on the edge of existence. Those who face malnutrition or starvation on a daily basis are not merely statistical entities, they are human beings in a desperate plight. In some cases the problem is far beyond their own control or influence, in other cases they or their fellow-countrymen have directly contributed to the predicament in which they find themselves. It is truly sad that all our efforts to combat hunger through the United Nations, through government aid programs, and through private relief organizations have not accomplished more. In the articles which follow, the situation will be examined critically, reasons will be given for our failure, and various solutions will be offered which we hope can produce the desired result.

We begin with the political aspects of the situation which are examined by two members of the federal government. These gentlemen are in unique positions to speak to the forces which have contributed to the hunger being experienced today throughout the world. They are also directly responsible for devising a workable solution to combat hunger. The Honorable E. (Kika) de la Garza, Congressman from Texas, is chairman of the House Agriculture Committee. He believes *The War on Hunger* is a war we must not lose.

"If we want a world with peace, freedom, justice and respect for life," he says, "we must move toward a world in which hunger is left to history." The short-term issue is how to deal with famine and the more insidious aspect of malnutrition. The answer quite simply is "the age-old obligation to share what we have with those who will die unless we act." Beyond this, our national and international policies must encourage farming and conservation of natural resources. Our policies must also emphasize the sharing of agricultural technology with the developing world, the promotion of trade among nations, and the acceptance of poverty as the prime cause of hunger. Four basic efforts have produced good results: 1) agricultural research and educational systems have been established in developing countries; 2) agricultural policy has encouraged production by giving farmers a chance to earn a profit; 3) new plant strains and technological advances have been introduced; and 4) "national leaders have recognized that a productive food system is an integrated whole" and have put the needed ingredients together in workable combinations. The long-term future prospects for eliminating hunger will depend on proper use of the world's soil and water resources, continuation of a strong research program, achievement of political stability in developing countries, and adoption of trade policies which will "spur economic growth and development."

Congressman de la Garza summarized his position as follows. "For the years immediately ahead, leaders must recognize that hunger is due much more to poverty in many developing areas than to the inability of world agriculture to produce enough food under normal circumstances. For the longer run, policies must also take into account the need to increase global productivity, to build the political institutions which promote increased productivity, and to protect the resources on which our productivity is based. . . If we lose (the war on hunger), the victim will be all mankind."

In Chapter II Mr. Peter McPherson speaks to the issue of hunger from the point of view of the Agency for International Development. He believes *The Hope of Africa* lies in the form of *A Green Revolution*. He has been directly involved in emergency relief efforts to provide food to drought–stricken parts of Africa. The problem can not be attributed to Mother Nature alone, because man himself has been responsible for "short-sighted agricultural practices and misuse of fragile lands, misguided centralized government planning, civil disorders, government policies that discriminate against farmers in pricing and marketing, and growing population pressures."

He cites the green revolution in India as an example of how one country has been able to cope with the situation. "It was a revolution brought about by science and technology, by education and training, by enlightened government policies, and by global concern coupled with the resolve that widespread, chronic hunger was a problem that could be solved." The success in India was due to a number of factors: incentive-pricing policies for farmers, new 'miracle' seeds of wheat and rice, irrigation systems and fertilizer production, establishment of agricultural universities, and the adaptability of farmers to new methods of cultivation. China has demonstrated similar progress, but Africa seems to lag behind.

There are encouraging signs, however, that indicate the revolution is underway in Africa as well. Hybrid seeds are being used in the Sudan, Zimbabwe, Niger, Mozambique, and Zambia. The International Crop Research Institute for the Semi-Arid Tropics and other Collaborative Research Support Programs funded by the Agency for International

Development have been successful in helping to increase yield of several staple crops such as sorghum, cowpeas, corn and cassavas. In addition, chemical compounds are being developed to combat insects and disease, which formerly wasted part of the food produced. More needs to be done, however, if the green revolution in Africa is to be completed. As A.I.D. continues to provide support, it will be guided by five principles.

First, explicit program objectives and priorities must be established so that resources can be focused on countries, commodities and research problems where the payoff is most likely to be high.

Second, integrated commodity and socio-economic research will be conducted to ensure that these on-station programs respond to the real concerns of African farmers.

Third, it is vital that there be sustained and stable support by U.S. and international institutions working on the problems which face many African nations.

Fourth, our commitment must be long-term with 20-25 years as the minimal acceptable planning period for assistance to African agriculture research systems and faculties of agriculture.

Fifth, we will continue to facilitate effective collaboration among outside donors with their diverse resources, and development of long-term national agricultural research strategies or programs.

Mr. McPherson concludes that "Technology alone cannot do the entire job. Institutional innovations, policy supports, and infrastructure investments must occur if agriculture is to develop and benefits are to spread widely among rural populations. However, without improved agricultural technologies, resulting from research, few development programs will move very far or have lasting effect. A green revolution for Africa can happen, if the world works together to make it happen."

Chapter III is devoted to a scientific analysis of *The Physiology of Hunger and Malnutrition*. Dr. Peter Pellett, Professor of Nutrition at the University of Massachusetts, first looks at nutrition on a global scale and then at the level of the individual. His thesis is that within every human being a direct but complex relationship exists among energy intake, energy expenditure and body stores. Furthermore, there appears to be a "causal relationship between malnutrition, poverty and economic development." In fact, "the widespread prevalency of hunger and malnutrition is usually the symptom of a very sick society." Women of childbearing age and young children are most vulnerable to major nutritional disorders such as protein–energy malnutrition, xeropthalmia, and goitre.

The actual assessment of nutritional status is difficult because data is not always available nor reliable. In any case, "amongst normal individuals requirements of many nutrients are affected by the nature of the diet, body size, activity, age, sex and physiological state." Dr. Pellett suggests that energy requirements thus be "specified for a pattern of work and discretionary activities appropriate to the various populations and subpopulations concerned." He goes on to say that "observations on the health of populations are also used to indicate nutritional status although such observations must be confirmed by food and nutrient intake data." For the individual, nutritional assessment includes anthropometric, biochemical and clinical studies."

Dr. Pellett concentrates primarily on starvation and malnutrition as reported in historical documents, such as from World War II prison camps, or in contemporary studies of persons denied sufficient nutrients. Marked changes in body weight, organ weight and body composition are found. "Two important adaptations to starvation are reduction in activity and reductions in basal metabolic rate," but these "may be different when growth is occurring." Furthermore, "almost all hormones are involved in the adaptations to food deprivation" and lead to "alterations in carbohydrate, protein, fat, water and electrolyte metabolism."

Since it is natural for a human being to want to survive, "all responses to starvation involve biochemical and physiological adaptations to ensure survival for as long as possible." The mechanism employed by the body involves conversion of carbohydrates, proteins and fats into useful metabolic components and energy. The process begins with carbohydrates being consumed and then goes on to the utilization of glycogen and fat. As starvation proceeds, however, gluconeogenesis and ketogenesis become more important. "In more advanced starvation. . . the major adaptive change is that the brain is able to use ketone bodies for fuel." This may or may not account for "intellectual and for emotional changes noted in starvation."

Finally, Dr. Pellett points out that "the documentation of a synergistic relationship between malnutrition and infection fundamentally changed the way in which potential solutions to the problems of world malnutrition were viewed." The availability of food and nutrients became closely linked with social and sanitation factors. He goes on to discuss "how infection influences the pathogenesis of protein–energy malnutrition" and the consequences of the "coincidental lack, in varying proportions, of protein and calories." Protein–energy malnutrition gives rise to "two distinct syndromes—at either end of the spectrum, marasmus and kwashiorkor." Both conditions involve infection.

In the epilogue, Dr. Pellett summarized the major changes which starvation causes "in the external actions and attributes of the body as well as in its internal functioning. All these changes can be considered as favoring survival in the face of a challenge to life." Moral and ethical dilemmas complicate our efforts to provide proper nutrition for people throughout the world and population growth continues to pose a long term threat to solving the problem. He concludes that "our scientific knowledge on the physiology and biochemistry of hunger and malnutrition—is sufficient to understand the majority of the major effects produced." The question is whether we have the capacity and the will to help those in need before it is too late.

*Reducing World Hunger: An Economist's View* is given in Chapter IV by Dr. Gale Johnson at the University of Chicago. His approach seems basically economic and hopeful. He cites "the modest improvements in food availability that have occurred over the past three decades" and goes on to say that "the adequacy of food supply is far more due to the mix of policies that governments follow than to the availability of natural resources of the vagaries of weather."

Food production in recent years has actually increased in all developing regions of the world, although with respect to Africa this favorable trend has been overtaken by growth in population as a whole. Nor do food supplies alone determine nutritional well-being. In twenty years Africa changed from being a net food exporter, to an importer of about 16% of total food supplies. This "made possible an increase in daily calorie consumption of about 20 percent compared to the decline of per capita food production of about 10 percent." In addition to food production, Dr. Johnson presents data on life expectancy as well as infant and child mortality. His conclusion is that "there has been significant improvement in health and nutritional status among the world's poor people" over the past two decades.

Dr. Johnson goes on to review projections for the future as presented in *The Global 2000 Report to the President* and *Agriculture: Toward 2000*. He considers carefully the underlying issues of supply and demand coupled with productivity growth. He points out that "these projections indicate a sharp slow down in growth of demand for cereals, oilseeds and meal with only a modest decline for milk;" this will be accompanied by a "reduction in the projected annual growth of cereal production" for the world as a whole. He concludes that "it is clearly possible to substantially improve per capita food consumption in the developing countries, though realizing the potential improvement will require significant changes in (individual) national policy."

Dr. Johnson then examines natural resource limitations such as the amount of additional land available for cultivation, energy supplies and fertilizer, water for irrigation and natural soil erosion. He believes that research and the use of modern technology, improved seeds, fertilizer, insecticides and disease controlling materials have made a tremendous impact on food production especially in the industrial countries. If these features of modern agriculture can be shared in an appropriate way, even more progress can be made in developing countries. This progress will be abetted by incentives for farmers, enlightened government policies and a politically supportive infrastructure.

In Dr. Johnson's opinion "poverty is the primary cause of hunger and malnutrition." While some parts of the world remain isolated and susceptible to crop failure, if supplies of food generally were "distributed more equitably, hunger and malnutrition could be eliminated." The production and distribution of this food, however, "depends to a much greater extent upon the actions of man than upon any restraints imposed by nature." China is cited as a convincing example of how changes in policy can produce amazing results. "The world possesses the resources—natural and human—to achieve a significant improvement in the nutrition of the people of the low income countries by the end of this century;" the question is whether we can make it happen.

In Chapter V. Dr. Garrett Hardin, professor emeritus of human ecology at the University of California–Santa Barbara, presents us with a discourse on *Lifeboat Ethics: A Radical Approach* and begins by taking the position that some problems do not have solutions. "We solved the problem of putting a man on the moon in less than a decade—but by now it should be clear that our progress towards solving 'the hunger problem' has been, if anything, negative: we get farther from the solution all the time." While we have thought that the marvels of technology would increase the supply of food sufficiently, we find that according to Koheleth's Principle "biological forces, unless curbed, increase the demand (for food) without limit." In other words, the more we feed the hungry, the more population will grow and the less food will be available for everyone.

In the past we have regarded hunger, poverty and injustice not as problems but rather as facts of life. Indeed, misfortunes such as pestilence, famine, wars and earthquakes were considered as blessings of a sort to overcrowded nations. But since "no healthy-minded person likes to be a witness to human suffering," we try to redistribute "the earth's goods among the human inhabitants thereof." While this solution may be applied effectively to small groups, the family for example, it can not be effective on a larger scale.

Dr. Hardin states his belief that the Christian–Marxist scheme of distribution "from each according to his ability, to each according to his needs," ultimately leads to disaster. "Among nations, as among people, irresponsible systems of sharing on the basis of need must be replaced by responsible systems of exchange on the basis of productivity." The concept of "Lifeboat Ethics" simply means that within society each separate operational unit must tailor "its demands to fit its resources." He goes on to say that "In the long run, meaningful responsibility minimizes suffering."

Compassion for the hungry prompts us to ask, "What can be done now?" Dr. Hardin uses Ethiopia as an example of a country with 36 million people, many of whom are starving. Given relief aid and a normal growth rate of 2.1 percent, "next year there will be 756,000 more Ethiopians who need to be fed." In subsequent years the number would be even higher. Under such circumstances "compassion is common, understanding rare."

Dr. Hardin then looks at the shortages confronting Ethiopians from an ecological point of view. They include food, crop land, pasture land, and forest land. The first is a "product" and the remaining three "production factors." While food may be supplied temporarily from outside sources, the "three production factors are over-strained in Ethiopia—the population has grown beyond the present carrying capacity of the land." The implication is that gifts of food may make things even worse than they are now.

Hence, population becomes another problem which needs to be solved. "It certainly seems irrational for a population that has already transgressed the carrying capacity (of the land) to continue to increase, thus further eroding the factors of production." The difficulty lies in making individual couples, who want to have children, realize that the interests of the country as a whole require limiting family size. "Unless this fundamental problem is attacked and solved," no amount of food aid nor technological advances in agriculture can overcome hunger.

In conclusion, Dr. Hardin characterized the future as bleak but not hopeless. He believes that "if we have the courage to base foreign aid policy on hard truths known to wise men and women at least since the time of Ecclesiastes," then developing countries will soon understand they must deal with the problems of population and food production themselves. By becoming self-reliant, these countries will have a far better chance of eliminating hunger than they do today.

Chapter VI is the final chapter in this collection of articles about hunger and moves us *Toward a Politics of Hope: Lessons from a Hungry World*. Frances Moore Lappé broaches the subject in terms of universal human feelings and draws heavily on her experience with the Institute for Food and Development Policy. She wants us to understand that "being hungry means making choices that no human being should ever have to make." When paying a mortgage means that peasants in El Salvador do not have money to feed their children, "there is the *anguish* of making impossible choices." In Nicaragua it was *grief*, when "being hungry means watching people you love die." In the Philippines and elsewhere, the exist-

9

ger and poverty are closely linked leading to a sense of *humili-*
...lly, in Guatemala people live in *fear,* because they may be
к.......anting to be independent of wealthy landowners. These are the
four emotions with which the hungry must cope and which we must try to
understand if we want to find solutions.

Ms. Lappé believes that hunger is the ultimate symbol of powerlessness. It is not a scarcity of natural resources which produces this powerlessness, because there is sufficient food, soil, and water throughout the
world to sustain life. It is rather a scarcity of democracy. Very simply,
fewer and fewer people control more and more land. This results in an
"increasing concentration of decision making. . . at the level of national
governments beholden to narrow elites." Finally, she laments the fact that
"a handful of corporations dominate world trade in most of the raw
commodities, which are the life–bloom of third world economies." Her
conclusion is that "at the root of hunger lies our own self–imposed powerlessness before economic dogma."

Two tenets of this economic dogma, the market and property rights,
are examined by Ms. Lappé in some detail. The market, she believes, does
not respond to needs but to money. Furthermore, the market is "blind to
the human and resource costs of the productive impetus it claims to foster" and "leads to the concentration of economic power—a concentration
that directly contributes to hunger and makes genuine political democracy
impossible." These factors must be overcome, if the market is to serve
human needs. The second major drawback of our economic dogmas is
"the absolute notion of unlimited private control of productive property."
In the opinion of Ms. Lappé, ownership of productive resources should
become "a cluster of rights and responsibilities in the service of our
values." This would apply to land as well as to the products of the land
and would ideally lead to a more equitable distribution of resources.

Ms. Lappé views our country's foreign policy as the most tragic consequence of this economic dogma. She believes that in the war between
capitalism and statism "our foreign aid becomes, not a channel through
which we can put ourselves on the side of hungry people, but a weapon
our government uses to make the world conform to its dogma." Low-
income countries get far less aid per capita than the more developed. In
order to make any headway against hunger, we must first admit "the
tragic failures in meeting human needs of both capitalism as we know it
and statism as we fear it." Then we must accept fundamental change as
necessary and inevitable. This will enable emerging peoples to determine
their own destiny free of both rigid dogmas—capitalism and statism.

She concludes with the hope that we will respond positively to the
need for greater maturity in dealing with "the very survival of life on
earth. . . Thus, a 'politics of hope' lies in our courage to unflinchingly
challenge the false gods of economic dogma. A 'politics of hope' lies in

garnering the confidence to trust in our deepest moral sensibilities, our deepest emotional intuitions about our connectedness to others' well-being. On this basis we will be able to challenge all dogma, demanding that it serve our values rather than continuing to contort our values so that dogma remains intact, while our fellow human beings starve in the midst of plenty."

Our heartfelt thanks go to all the authors who responded so willingly to the request that they participate in the Bristol–Myers lecture series at the University of Evansville. They have made a truly remarkable contribution to our understanding of *Global Hunger: A Look at the Problem and Potential Solutions.* We are gratified to have played a part in the publication of these papers and recommend that the reader take the time to fully absorb the diverse and insightful points of view assembled here.


Malcolm H. Forbes
Vice President for Academic Affairs
University of Evansville

Lois J. Merrill
Dean, School of Nursing
and Health Sciences
University of Evansville

# THE WAR ON HUNGER: THE WAR WE MUST NOT LOSE

## E. (Kika) de la Garza

World hunger has been described for decades by students and leaders in many countries as a challenge we all face. The actions we take to meet this challenge could then be called a "war on hunger." If you accept this description, and I believe you should, you must also regard what lies ahead as a war that mankind cannot afford to lose. To open a review of this kind, we should first define the areas we want to examine. I suggest that we build a framework for our discussion by looking at the universal values that virtually every society on the face of the earth promotes, or claims to promote.

We want a world that lives in peace, but hunger and peace do not co-exist happily or for long periods. We want a world society that respects life, but hunger weakens life, malnutrition tears down the quality of life and starvation ends life. We want a world in which there is freedom both for nations and for individuals, but freedom, like peace, does not co-exist easily with continuing hunger and malnutrition. History shows that desperate, hungry people can too often be persuaded to trade freedom for bread. Finally, we want a world of justice, but societies which are starving may not be free and peaceful, and nations which are not free and peaceful may not deal justly with their people and their neighbors.

If we accept these as universal values and if we want a world with peace, freedom, justice and respect for life, we must move toward a world in which hunger is left to history. That is the goal, but we probably will not reach that goal within the lifetime of anyone living today. The most important thing, however, is not how far we have to go but rather, whether we are making decent progress in the right direction.

To measure the distance we have to go, and to measure the pace at which we are making progress, we have to divide the problem into two parts. There is, first, the question of hunger and malnutrition around the world today, for example, the famine crises in Africa and the gap between diets and health needs in other developing countries. These are problems for today, tomorrow and next year, and they demand a particular kind of response. In addition, however, we must also define the problem of feeding the population of the expanded world of the next century, and I suggest that this will require another and distinctly different kind of response.

**Short Term Issues**

In one way, the problem of hunger in the world today is something new for mankind. Through much of man's history, hunger was chronic for much of the population because people could not grow enough food. We simply did not have the knowledge needed to produce enough for even the comparatively small populations of earlier times. For thousands of years, the human race lived almost continually on the ragged edge of hunger. Food supplies were enough to keep people alive in good years, but weather problems which today would be minor factors could produce widespread famine and death. For the poor, hunger was a regular companion in the good years as well as in the bad years.

The problem of hunger in the world of 1985, however, is not based on our inability to produce enough food. Agricultural science has produced a body of science and technology that can, if it is used properly around the world, provide the food the world needs for today's population. The primary cause of hunger today, wherever it exists, is a combination of poverty and a failure that is essentially a political issue—a failure in some parts of the world to make proper use of existing natural, technological and economic resources.

It may sound strange, at a time when the sights and sounds of the tragic famines in some parts of Africa are still fresh, to talk about the progress that has been made in this century, particularly in the years since the end of World War II. Yet that progress is very real. A recent report from the House of Representatives Select Committee on Hunger points out that between 1950 and 1980, life expectancy in developing countries increased by about 40 percent, a gain that took two full centuries to achieve in the developed world. In the developing nations, death rates for children have been cut in half during the past two decades, providing another sign of progress that is based on a number of factors but which cannot take place without gains in food.

The record on what has been done to improve the food supply around the world is impressive. Since the 1950's, food production in developing countries in the world as a whole has increased by an average of about 3 percent a year which is a better record than we had in the developed nations during the same period. Even when one takes into account the fact that population in the developing nations has nearly doubled during the past three decades, the gains in food supply remain. The Secretary of Agriculture testified before the House Agriculture Committee last year that the average consumption of calories per person around the world has risen since 1960 and the per capita food supply has risen in most developing countries.

The problem is, however, that this progress has not been uniform. The figures for all developing countries as a group do not tell us that some of them are not sharing in the gains. The chief problem area is Africa where per capita food production has been going down in recent years, partly because of drought and partly because of other factors which will be examined later.

When we look at the issue of hunger in the world today, we should keep all these changes in mind. We have come a long way toward making hunger a part of history, but we still have a long way to go.For example, food and development agencies around the world have estimated the number of hungry people around the globe today at anywhere between 450 million and 1.3 billion. The numbers can vary widely, in part because it is very hard to get experts to agree on just what constitutes "hunger" for individuals. The United Nations Food and Agriculture Organization estimates the number of undernourished people in the world today at nearly 500 million, and world health statistics indicate that about one in every three children in Africa and parts of Asia is afflicted by either moderate or severe malnutrition.

I do not intend to try to weigh the merits of all these efforts to measure the scope and depth of the problem of world hunger today. The simple fact is that no matter whose figures are correct, there are too many people who do not get enough to eat.The question is not whether something must be done. The question is what must be done, how it should be done, and who should be doing it.

The first answer should deal with the issue of meeting the challenge of famine as it exists today. This is the easiest of all the questions we have to face in this decade. The answer is clear and simple. The world must provide the emergency food supplies needed to keep men, women and children alive through the current crisis. The longer-term answers are more complicated and more difficult, but the people of some parts of Africa will not live to take part in the long-range solutions if they do not get emergency food aid this year.

So, for the short range, the answer to famine is the answer mankind has always known. It is the age-old obligation to share what we have with those who will die unless we act.It should not need saying, but this is not an obligation for the United States alone, or for the developed nations alone. As a nation, we have been more than generous over the years and we have followed that tradition in the African crisis. The same can be said for many other nations, but we must make it part of the record that the obligation to help extends to all nations and all peoples who can make any contribution, large or small, in shipments of food or medical supplies or in aid for buying and distributing those supplies.

Beyond the famine question we must deal with the bundle of issues involved in the hunger problem, and this is a more difficult and dangerous area. It is when we move on to the issues of chronic hunger and malnutrition that the complexity of the problem increases. The solutions become more deeply involved in political and economic choices, and the dangers of making easy and wrong decisions become greater.

It is not really hard, in the political sense, to produce a sense of national and international agreement to deal with a famine. The whole world reads about death and disease in the drought areas. Hundreds of millions of people around the world see for themselves, on television screens, the sights and sounds of death and disease in dozens of African villages and refugee camps. There is a shared sense that something must be done, and the things that must be done are familiar responses which we have all made before.

But chronic hunger and malnutrition are something else. Chronic malnutrition does not produce dramatic news stories or television pictures of dying children and mothers lying in the dust. The House of Representatives Hunger Committee report put it this way: "The chronic lack of enough to eat leads to higher death rates, stunted physical and mental development in children, anemia, lassitude. . . and a lower quality of life. Hungry people become sick more often, miss more days of work, and are able to take advantage of fewer opportunities." These are deep and critical problems, but they do not produce at any one time the hot drama that holds the public attention and produces a national or international consensus that something must be done.

Hunger and malnutrition can kill, but the killing is done quietly, even subtly. A child dying of a disease that he might resist if his diet had been good is a statistic, not a dramatic five minutes on the evening news. A woman whose life is shortened by 10 years because of a lifetime of poor nutrition is another statistic, not a symbol that rallies millions of people to contribute to relief funds.

So we come down to this: the shared national and international sense of outrage at the sight of obvious famine is not there, at least not to the same degree, when we deal with the continuing problem of hunger and malnutrition. Without that sense of outrage, we need to find some other way to create a force that will drive a continuing and effective national and international attack on hunger and malnutrition. Since we do not have the fire of a famine situation to generate public support for the policies that must be followed, we are going to have to rely on a determination to make international assistance programs of all kinds contribute effectively to wiping out hunger.

I am not suggesting a really new policy. National leaders and academic experts in many countries have been saying for years that food assistance programs, as desirable and necessary as they are in most cases, can cause problems for the future if they are poorly designed. For example, the Secretary of Agriculture had this to say in testimony in 1983 before the house agriculture committee:

A strong U.S. commitment to food aid is essential, but it will not end hunger and malnutrition in the developing world. For one thing, problems with storage, transportation and distribution make it hard to get food aid to those most in need. They also make it difficult for developing nations to conserve their supplies. In Africa, post-harvest losses can run as high as 60 percent. We must prevent food aid from undermining agricultural development in recipient countries and fostering dependence instead of self-reliance. Real food security and a decline in hunger rest in helping developing countries grow more food and storing and distributing it more effectively. Helping their agricultural economies will also allow them to earn enough to import more food.

National and international leaders have been making similar statements for many years. Now, I think we may need something more. We may need a real commitment to take this perfectly sound policy with total seriousness. I am emphatically *not* saying that we should deny food to starving people unless they agree to follow policies geared to long-range goals. I *am* saying that wherever food aid and similar assistance from our country and others are geared to development efforts rather than immediate famine problems, we must have an international drive to concentrate on the world's real needs.

Specifically, this means we and other national and international aid providers should insist to the greatest extent possible that food aid will not be used to raise prices to levels at which local farmers are driven out of business.Furthermore, we should use every legitimate means to persuade developing nations that policies which protect natural resources are better than policies that produce deserts. And we should be ready to say that aid keyed to unsound policies is not in the interests of either party.

We should, in summary, make sure that our government and all other national and international assistance providers operate under the principle laid down in September, 1984, by C. Payne Lucas, the executive director of the agency called Africare: "It is critical that we examine the relationship of emergency food relief, concessionary food sales and food-for-work programs in terms of whether they promote or retard long-term agricultural self-reliance." This is not an easy policy to follow.The years of development and anti-hunger programs since World War II have taught us that promoting agricultural growth sometimes requires tough choices in developing countries, choices that not all countries make correctly.

The example of Africa is, perhaps, the best justification for following an international policy which tries to make sure that efforts to feed people today do not result in long-term losses in the war on hunger. The Congressional Office of Technology Assessment underlines this point in its December, 1984, report entitled "Africa Tomorrow." The report notes that:

> Government policies in most African countries have adversely affected food production, including: an urban bias in development strategies, a lack of attention to low-resource farmers (the base of the food production system), a lack of price incentives for farmers to grow food crops, often inappropriate and inefficient government involvement in the marketing and distribution of agricultural inputs and outputs, and often inappropriate import and fiscal policies.

Along with effective programs of development, we must recognize that any real effort to reduce world hunger levels over the next few decades will require coordinated action in a number of other areas. First, we will need to continue food aid programs, both as part of the development process and as a humanitarian effort to improve the diets of needy people. This means that the food for peace program, which Congress launched more than 30 years ago, must continue with increased emphasis on making sure that it does not depress agriculture in the developing world.

—Secondly, we will need to continue sharing argricultural technology with the developing world. There will have to be increased emphasis on what many experts have told us is the greatest pitfall in technology transfers, the danger of trying to transfer technologies that do not really fit the needs and conditions of the host countries.

—Third, we will need to promote trade policies which take full account of the needs of American farmers to get fair access to world markets, but which also give developing nations a chance to earn the money they need to buy from us and other developed countries. A concern for improving agriculture in the third world does not necessarily mean those countries will buy less from the American farmer. It may, on the contrary, make them better cash customers for many of our farm products as their income levels increase.

Finally, perhaps as important as any other single factor, we will need to build into our policymaking process an acceptance of the fact that the prime cause of hunger in the world today is poverty.


**Poverty the Root Cause**

Just a few short years ago, in March of 1980, a Presidential Commission on World Hunger filed a report stating that "of all the challenges facing the world today, agreement by the nations of the world on the actions required of all countries to eliminate hunger may be the most important, and may also provide the most promising basis for other international actions to assure world peace." The Commission went on to say that the United States should "make the elimination of hunger the primary focus of its relationships with the developing world beginning with the decade of the 1980's." When it came to the question of just what needs to be done to help improve diets around the world, the Commission's answer was clear. It amounts to this: when poor people become less poor, they will be less hungry.

The Commission's language on this crucial point is worth repeating, because it remains a key to the development of anti-hunger policy today and in the years ahead. The report said: "World hunger has many related causes, some of which result from scientific, technical and logistical problems. However, the central and most intransigent cause is poverty. Hunger, therefore, is primarily a political, economic, and social problem. The Commission concurs with the National Academy of Sciences that 'in most countries, social, economic and political measures not directly related to food are necessary to reduce malnutrition and improve health.' "

If policymakers accept the fact that poverty is one of the basic causes of world hunger problems, they automatically accept another concept, namely the idea that the attack on hunger must include more than food, and more than efforts to help farmers grow increasing supplies of food. The attack on hunger must also be broad enough to include improvements in health care, in education, in all the things that go to make up a better standard of living, and in the ability of families in developing nations to earn more income.

## Effective Solutions

In spite of the fact that there is more hunger in the world today than we want to accept, most students recognize that there have been success stories. There are nations where, during the last few decades of American and international aid programs, we have seen real progress toward bringing the problem under control. If we want to extend that progress into regions and countries which are still lagging, we should look briefly at what factors have helped to produce good results.

1. Some developing nations, with the help of the United States and other countries, have built agricultural research and educational systems. These new or improved research and educational institutions, like the network of agricultural colleges created in India with the cooperation of American universities, have been able to find workable solutions adapted to local needs and conditions, and to spread information to producers.

2. In some of the successful developing nations, progress has been spurred because individual farmers and other private enterprise operators in agriculture have been given a chance to earn a profit. Never underestimate the power of the profit motive in persuading human beings to provide goods for others.

3. Research by international agencies has produced breakthroughs like the grains that touched off the so-called green revolution in parts of Asia and Latin America. The lesson here is that new plant and technology discoveries work well when they are successfully adapted to the areas where they are introduced.

4. In areas where development has been successful, it has usually been because national leaders recognized that a productive food system is an integrated whole. It is an industry that stretches from input suppliers of many kinds on one hand, to farms and ranches and on to providers of transportation, storage, processing and distribution services. The precise mix that works best varies from country to country, and even within countries, but the success stories come when leaders recognize the needed ingredients and put them together in workable combinations.

If these four basic factors can be put to work in the developing countries, we could hope for more substantial progress in the coming decades.In Africa, the need for a realistic approach to anti-hunger policy is especially clear. This region has more obstacles with which to cope than most others in its effort to provide a decent standard of living for its people. The area has low and erratic rainfall, short growing seasons, low-quality soil in many areas, and a tremendous problem of population pressure on the land. Given these obstacles, it will take heroic efforts and a long period of dedicated work to bring African incomes and productivity up to levels that meet the real needs of the continent's peoples.

**The Longer View**

In November of 1974, a World Food Conference convened in Rome to discuss the same issues we are looking at here today. I was at the time the Chairman of a House Subcommittee which had some responsibilities in the area of world agriculture, so I attended that conference. I recall that when the conference ended, it left behind this declaration:

> All governments should accept the removal of the scourge of hunger and malnutrition. . . as the objective of the international community as a whole, and accept the goal that within a decade, no child will go to bed hungry, that no family will fear for its next day's bread, and that no human being's future and capacities will be stunted by malnutrition.

The decade mentioned in the world food conference statement has now gone by. The world made some progress in those years, but in 1984 and 1985 Sub-Saharan Africa was facing its second severe food crisis in a little over a decade. The world has not yet reached the stage at which no family is worried about having enough to eat tomorrow morning.

I cannot predict when we will reach the goal set by the food conference in 1974. I am not interested in setting a specific date, because any exercise of that kind would be based only on hope and guesswork, not on knowledge and confidence. What I can do with confidence is to predict that even if we bring the number of hungry people in the world down to nearly zero in the near term—that is, between now and the end of the century—the war against hunger will not be over. The job of providing for the generations of the 21st century and beyond is likely to be even more challenging than the massive job which confronts the world today.

Most of the discussion of world hunger policy in recent years has dealt with what I have classified as the near-term problem. We have examined carefully the issues involving what must be done to improve diets and food supplies between now and the year 2000. As important as these issues are, however, I hope that scholars and policy officials will not put a 15- year fence around their studies. This country and the world is going to need a solid basis of study and debate for the decisions nations will make in the 21st century.

Some of the issues that will face those concerned about world hunger in the next century may deal with matters that we know little or nothing about today. Nobody can say today just what kinds of political, economic or moral choices will be forced on the world by the scientific and technological discoveries of the next few decades. In some cases, however, the policy areas that will be critical to the decisions of the next century are visible now because they will grow out of the same issues on which leaders must concentrate during the years immediately ahead.

Those areas in which decisions made during the next decade or two will have great impact on the long-term future include the following:

NATURAL RESOURCES The world's soil and water resources are the basic foundations for the food supply of the future. If the human race is going to feed and clothe itself in the 21st century, you and I will have to see to it that the basic resources are in place. The 1980 Commission on World Hunger was correct when it pointed out that, "there can be no lasting solution to the world hunger problem if the world persists in current practices which have already led to increasingly serious degradation of soils, grasslands, water resources, forests and fisheries." The grim story of the spread of the desert in Africa is perhaps the most visible current sign of this problem. It would be a mistake, however, to assume that the developing world is the only region where preservation and potential repair of natural resources is an important issue for 21st century food policy. Our own country has a conservation problem. We are still losing soils at a rate that is too great to accept if there is real concern about the needs of our grandchildren. A sound conservation policy for the United States during the next decade will be a key building block for the anti-hunger policy of the next century.

RESEARCH A strong research program will be essential in the future, as it has been in the past, to any effort to deal with world hunger. Research cannot provide the economic sense of the political will needed to guide nations along the path to a world where hunger is not a major fact of life. But without research, policymakers will not have the tools needed to solve the problems the world will face.

POLITICAL STABILITY One of the factors that helps promote food security is political stability. It should be obvious that stable and free regions are far more able to concentrate their energies on meeting the basic human needs of their people than are countries where political and social turmoil is the rule. It may be argued that authoritarian governments would be better able to make hard decisions involving resources and development, but I believe there are equal or greater risks that authoritarian governments would tend to make decisions aimed at preserving their own powers. For this reason, I am concerned that the better and more lasting moves toward development will come from democratic societies.

TRADE POLICY Many people concerned with world hunger issues tend to forget how much the opportunity to trade can spur economic growth and development. Policies which move toward a reduction in international trade barriers will be important not only in the near term but also for the longer run, because the existence of opportunities for trade will encourage the development of agricultural systems best suited to the resources and special conditions of each nation. A system in which countries specialize in the things they produce most efficiently would be a great spur to the kind of development needed in the 21st century.

## Summary

The issue of world hunger is one which affects virtually every aspect of international affairs today, and will continue to play a key role in shaping the world of the future. The hunger problem is not easy to understand or to explain. It is built of a complex web of political, historical, cultural and economic circumstances. It is both easy and dangerous to misread the causes and potential solutions to the problem. The United States and other nations, working alone sometimes and together through international agencies, have made progress in recent decades toward reducing the amount of hunger in the world. However, the number of people who remain malnourished is still unacceptably high in total and dangerously high in some regions, such as parts of Africa.

Many of the policies and programs followed during the past few decades in fighting hunger have achieved good results and should be continued. These include food assistance programs such as the American Food for Peace Program, and development assistance programs like many of the foreign aid operations carried on by our own government and by some United Nations efforts like the world food program. One of the most promising steps in recent years has been the work of the Board for International Food and Economic Development, an agency which I helped bring into existence a few years ago. This board works to match the expertise and talents of American universities with the needs of individual developing countries which want to improve their own systems of agricultural extension.

It would be impossible to catalog all the domestic and international programs that have been used, sometimes effectively, sometimes not, in the effort to reduce and eventually eliminate hunger. Fortunately, these efforts have at least moved us some distance ahead in the campaign, and I strongly urge that our national policy continue to put strong emphasis on the problem. In addition, I believe that national anti-hunger policy should continue to reserve a strong role for the many private voluntary agencies which mobilize citizen support for anti-hunger activities. The policy should also continue to place strong emphasis on the role of private enterprise in agricultural development.

In viewing the hunger problem, we must be careful to distinguish between immediate, crisis-style famine relief needs and the problems of reducing and hopefully eliminating chronic hunger and malnutrition. To reduce chronic hunger, both in the comparatively short time remaining in this century and in the longer run into the 21st century, national and international leaders must begin by analyzing the causes of hunger and then must tailor policies to deal with those causes. For the years immediately ahead, leaders must recognize that hunger is due much more to poverty in many developing areas than to the inability of world agriculture to produce enough food under normal circumstances. For the longer run, policies must also take into account the need to increase global productivity, to build the political institutions which promote increased productivity, and to protect the resources on which our productivity is based.

Finally, our policies for the future must take serious account of future trends in population. It does not need saying that the amount of food the world needs depends heavily on the size of the population in coming years. Population growth trends have moderated in developed countries and in many developing areas as well. Governments in all parts of the world are aware of the importance of the people side of the food-population equation. I am certain that people as well as food will and must continue to be a factor in policymaking for the war against hunger, which as I have said, is the "WAR WE CANNOT LOSE." If we lose, the victim will be all mankind.

Representative E. (Kika) de la Garza, member of Congress, 15th district, Texas since 1965 has served continuously since that time on the House of Representatives Agriculture Committee. He has served as chairman of that committee since 1981, and has also served as Chairman of the Subcommittee on Department Operations, Research and Foreign Agriculture. He has been active in promoting better relations with both the developing world and other major trading nations, and in the development of research programs needed to permit American agriculture to meet growing domestic and world needs.

# THE HOPE OF AFRICA: THE GREEN REVOLUTION

M. Peter McPherson

In Ethiopoia and other African countries I have seen firsthand the human tragedy unfolding there. Millions of people are at risk of starvation. Many thousands have already died in the famine of the past year. If it were not for the emergency food, water, and medicines that have been pouring into these African countries, thousands more would have perished.

This year the United States will provide over three million tons of food for Africa. President Reagan has committed over one billion dollars in food and emergency assistance for Africa, or approximately one-half of the estimated need for this year. To give an idea of the magnitude of the U.S. contribution, if it were packed into fifty pound bags placed end-to-end, they would go around the world twice.

I have seen children being fed with our food and I have heard the silence of starvation change to the laughter of nourished babies. I can assure you that the help that we are giving is being properly used to meet the short-term needs of the hungry.

The dimensions of this tragedy are mind-boggling. Not only in terms of lives threatened or lost, but also in terms of why it happened. The famine is largely man-made and only partly the work of Mother Nature. The drought itself, of course, was Mother Nature's doing. But other problems were created by man:

> shortsighted agricultural practices and misuse of fragile
> lands;
> misguided centralized government planning;
> civil disorders;
> government policies that discriminate against farmers
> in pricing and marketing;
> growing population pressures.

In most of the world per capita food production has risen continuously in recent years. But in Africa it has fallen each year during the past twenty years. At the Agency for International Development (A.I.D.) we believe this decline can, and must, be reversed.

The experience of recent history clearly shows it can be done. The conditions in Africa today are similar to those in India a fairly short time ago. As recently as the 1960's, India was considered by many as beyond hope, the basket case of the world. Hunger was everywhere. Starvation was common.

But then a revolution began. It was a revolution brought about by science and technology, by education and training, by enlightened government policies, and by global concern coupled with the resolve that widespread, chronic hunger was a problem that could be solved.

In India:

> Political leaders fashioned incentive—pricing policies for farmers.
>
> Scientists in international research centers and national centers developed new 'miracle' seeds of wheat and rice.
>
> Government policy makers, private industrialists and farmers cooperated to increase production and use of fertilizers and irrigation systems.
>
> Farmers exhibited the willingness to adapt to new methods of cultivation and to share their experience with their neighbors.

As a result, rice production has tripled, wheat production has increased sevenfold, and other food products have followed the rising tide of production.

Today, while hunger and malnutrition are far from conquered in India, widespread famine has been banished. In many parts of the world, there has been a 'green revolution'-a revolution of research, development, technology transfer, institution building, incentives, and, policy reform.

As an another example, in China food supplies lagged behind population growth until agricultural policies were reversed in 1979. The old communal farms were changed, land was leased to families and small groups, and farm price incentives were increased. The new technology of miracle rice became available in the last several years. In brief, production has dramatically increased. Clearly, the dramatic progress in many parts of the world attests to what the world scientific community, farmers, and governments can accomplish.

Let us turn now to Africa. Africa is at an earlier stage of development than other regions, and increasing agricultural production is more difficult. Vast areas have only rudimentary transportation networks, and this inhibits marketing agricultural surpluses and supplying production inputs. Water, a scarce commodity in Africa, is poorly utilized. Shortages of foreign exchange limit imports vital to expanded production.

Our foreign assistance program is currently helping to overcome these production constraints by providing substantial quantities of fertilizer and agricultural implements, extending Africa's rural road network, and expanding the continent's fledgling irrigation systems. In all, A.I.D. projects and commodities worth more than $250 million are focused on the task of strengthening African production systems. Improvement will require equally extensive efforts in agricultural research, in strengthening the human resource and institutional base, and in encouraging policy reform. I believe the time is right for a 'green revolution' in Africa. The most promising sign is the recent willingness of some African leaders to reform their economic and agricultural policies.

Some observers have argued that Africa isn't suitable for the irrigation systems needed to grow those original 'miracle' seeds. They agree that although there is land that could be irrigated in several African river basins, the cost is high and the area is not large compared to the total needs, and they are correct. To meet Africa's food needs a different approach is required. A green revolution for Africa will not be measured in huge areas of irrigated fields. Rather, it will mean dramatic increases in productivity in the rainfed crops and the livestock that most Africans now produce and consume: corn, sorghum, millet, cassava, beans, milk and meat.

For many of these crops basic scientific understanding is limited. A continuing agricultural research effort is therefore essential. In an inhospitable agricultural environment, new technologies like those that transformed Asian agriculture are more difficult to develop. Several important breakthroughs will be necessary given the great variance in African climates and soils.

Systematic international and national-level efforts to develop food crop technologies for most of Africa are relatively recent. As a major contributor to these efforts, A.I.D. is supporting intensive agricultural research programs in 25 African countries. The portfolio of programs now totals more than $350 million. An additional $100 million is now being committed to new research efforts this coming year. Already, new technologies in maize, sorghum, tubers and other crops are emerging.

Research supported by A.I.D. has produced a new sorghum hybrid which promises to help ease the chronic food shortages that plague much of Africa. Under drought conditions, the new sorghum has yields of 150 percent over traditional varieties. Collaborative research by the A.I.D. supported International Crop Research Institute for the Semi-Arid Tropics (ICRISAT) and the Agricultural Research Corporation that began in 1977 led to the release in January 1983 of the first commercial sorghum hybrid in the Sudan. The new hybrid, Hageen Dura-1 (Arabic for Hybrid Sorghum #1), is high-yielding, early maturing, adapted to both irrigated and rainfed locations, and producible by conventional hybridization techniques. It also possesses acceptable milling and local food quality characteristics. To ensure that this new hybrid would be utilized by Sudanese farmers, the A.I.D.-funded Sorghum/Millet Collaborative Research Support Program (CRSP) and the A.I.D. Mission in Khartoum have cooperated in a pilot project to multiply and distribute good quality seed of the new hybrid. This project will help to ensure adequate supplies of seed during the transition period from government production and distribution to private production and marketing. If, as is now projected, 25 percent of Sudan's current sorghum acreage is planted to the new hybrid by the end of the decade, that could double total sorghum production and reduce future food deficits in the Sudan. If further tests show that this new cultivar and similar hybrids can perform well in other African countries, the impact on nutrition and human welfare in Africa will be dramatic.

The cowpea, *Vigna unguiculata,* is one of the most commonly grown food grain legumes, particularly in Africa and Latin America. It is a dietary staple of both the urban and rural poor. Frequently, cowpeas are relegated to the hotter and drier parts of a country, since it is one of the few crops that will tolerate such conditions. Yields, however, are then correspondingly lower. Recently, an A.I.D.-supported Collaborative Research Support Program on beans and cowpeas has developed drought-resistant, high–yielding lines by crossing lines of cowpeas from California and Senegal. Tests over a three–year period in unusually dry conditions in the semi-arid zone of Senegal proved that the new lines could produce two to four times the average yield of the traditional lines, even under these extremely adverse conditions. Senegalese scientists are now testing these cowpeas on farmers' fields. Cooperative linkages between the CRSP and international agricultural research centers will extend the outputs of this project to other parts of Africa.

In Zimbabwe, small-scale farmers, largely Black, have achieved substantial increases in corn production despite three years of drought. This is the result of superior hybrid seed varieties researched and developed over several years. In Niger, new white corn varieties appear to produce several times the usual yields. In Nigeria, a new cassava variety appears to outyield local strains by as much as 1,800 percent!

New miracle seeds are not the only thing that scientists are discovering. U.S. scientists have discovered a protozoan pest that kills grasshoppers. It may be able to be spread among the billions of grasshoppers that infest West Africa.

A new vaccine against a debilitating cattle disease known as East Coast Fever has been developed. The vaccine was developed by scientists at the International Laboratory for Research on Animal Diseases (ILRAD) (one of the International Agricultural Centers to which A.I.D. is a major donor) after years of research on the disease. Formerly, the only control for East Coast Fever was costly dipping and spraying, which had to be repeated on a regular basis. Immunization will provide economical and effective control within the means of the average African farmer. Vaccination trials to assess the efficacy of the serum in the field are currently being conducted in a number of African countries, jointly run by ILRAD and national research program scientists. If the trials are as successful as hoped, commercial production and distribution of the vaccine will begin.

These examples are encouraging. They are, however, only the first steps in a long and complex journey toward the goal of food self–reliance in Africa. At A.I.D., we recognize that research and the creation of support mechanisms requires a long–term commitment. We pledge our support for this goal in Africa for as long as it takes.

A.I.D. has developed a long–term plan to strengthen the contribution of agricultural science and technology to achieve food self—reliance in Africa. Emphasis will be given to strenghtening agricultural research capabilities and the faculties of agriculture.

In order to make the most effective use of Agency financial and human resources, criteria are needed to guide choices among the countries and commodities to support. Twenty to 25 years of continuous support are required to build the research and human capital base to achieve desired results. A.I.D.'s effort will, therefore, draw on the resources of the entire Agency-Missions, the Africa Bureau, and A.I.D. Washington central bureaus-working with African countries and other donors in a sustained, cooperative, focused program. National agricultural research systems will be strengthened in approximately eight core countries. Strong adaptive research capacities will be built in neighboring countries to enable local scientists to screen and borrow technologies and adapt them to local environments. Networks will link national systems, international agricultural research centers (IARCs), regional research programs, collaborative research support programs (CRSPs), centrally-funded projects, and other-donor assistance on selected, high-priority topics. Four to six faculties of agriculture will be selected initially for long-term assistance.

For the past 15 years or more, A.I.D. and other donors have attempted to reverse the declining per capita food production in sub-Sahara Africa. The Agency has been investing in agricultural research capacity development by providing technical assistance, training, and other physical support to national research institutions. This support has been given to some 25 African nations addressing scores of different commodity and factor-specific research problems. However, these investments have been erratic and the results have been disappointing because they have not built adequate African agricultural research capacity nor have they generated the farmer-relevant technology needed.

A.I.D.'s new plan reflects a rethinking of approaches to technology and manpower development in Africa to improve the effectiveness of investments in agricultural research and faculties of agriculture. Our past experience in Africa provides a strong guidance for shaping future investments. The following broad points are crucial:

We need explicit objectives for agricultural research.

We need focused program priorities to emphasize

selected countries, commodities, and problems.

We need to give greater support to commodity research.

We need to concentrate on food crop research, recognizing that food crop production can contribute significantly to income and export growth.

We need to improve the complementarity among A.I.D.'s various mechanisms for undertaking investments in agricultural research and faculties of agriculture.

We need to make a long-term commitment toward the development of agricultural research and higher education.

We need to assist countries to develop their management and administration capabilities in research.

We need to be willing to finance a portion of recurrent costs of research programs and faculties of agriculture, where appropriate.

We need to cooperate with other donors in planning and carrying out these investments.

**Need for Clear Objectives:** A.I.D.'s overall objective is to assist African countries to develop improved technologies for farmers which can increase agricultural production and incomes. Africa's nations differ substantially with regard to population, size, economic stability, commitment to agricultural development, institutional capacity, and a number of other factors that influence a nation's ability to benefit from donor assistance. Moreover, some countries are simply too small or too resource-poor to provide the base needed to develop and sustain full-fledged agricultural research systems. In recognition of this, A.I.D. intends to pursue a dual strategy. In those countries having the natural and economic base to develop basic and adaptive research, the agency will make investments to build this capacity so that the technology generated can be used at home and transferred through networks to neighboring countries. In a second group of countries that lacks the economic resource base to develop and finance a large national agricultural research service, investments will be made to strengthen the manpower capacity of the research service to borrow technologies generated in other countries and research centers, and to adapt the technologies to local needs and conditions.

**Research Networks:** Because of the large number of small countries in Africa, it is not cost-effective to approach agricultural research problems entirely on a country-by-country basis. Most of the national agricultural research systems in small countries are thinly staffed and poorly financed. Agricultural research is costly. A "critical mass" of scientists is needed to produce new knowledge through basic and applied research. In many cases they are not always available at the national level. It is, however, possible to build a critical mass of scientists through the collective joining of scientific manpower in the small countries and focusing their work on a specific problem. Problems that transcend national borders or even regional groupings often may be addressed more effectively by institutions that are interregional or global in nature. These institutions, in turn, can provide support for national programs in specific program areas.

A.I.D. will facilitate agricultural research cooperation on a zonal basis to complement national research efforts. The major national research institutions producing new technologies will be encouraged to help implement collaborative networks with other national research systems as well as with regional and international research centers. These collaborative networks will be inter-country working relationships, facilitating the planning and coordination of research and the backstopping of national programs. In most instances, the IARCs will take a leadership role in development of networks. In some cases, it may be necessary to support small African regional institutions to coordinate with IACRs to lead network development. Over time, strong African national agricultural research systems must assume leadership roles in these scientific networks.

The development of networks in sub-Saharan Africa will be designed to plan strategic components of research to solve problems, foster the exchange of scientific knowledge, and facilitate cost-effectiveness. They will not be means for building large operational staffs or physical facilities. Several areas are especially promising for collaborative networks. On-farm research with a farming systems perspective is one of these. In addition, we plan to support, initially, four to six commodity networks, each in one or more zones. The following appear to have highest potential:

> Maize—Eastern Highlands, Western Coastal, Zaire Basin, and Southern Zones.
> Sorghum and Millet—Southern, Sahelian, Sudanisan, and Eastern Highlands Zones.
> Roots and Tubers—Zaire Basin and Western Coastal Zones.
> Edible Legumes (particularly beans and cowpeas)— Eastern Highlands, Western Coastal, and Sahelian Zones.
> Upland Rice—Western Coastal Zone and Madagascar.
> Forages in Mixed Farming Systems—Sahelian, Sudanian, Eastern Highlands, and Southern Zones.

**Need for Donor Cooperation:** With many donors working in Africa, duplication of effort is a serious problem. If donors meet prior to project planning, conflicts of interest and duplication of effort can be minimized.

Also, donors can work together and share costs in order to allocate sufficient donor resources to large-scale problems. For example, a logical division of resources would be for the United States to use its grant funds for technical assistance and training to complement financing from other donors for buildings, other infrastructure, and equipment. Similarly, the United States can direct support to research on food crops to complement research assistance on traditional export crops by European donors or the private sector. Special initiatives will be undertaken by A.I.D. Missions to work with and strenghten collaborative efforts among countries. The responsibility to nurture regional collaboration is of primary importance to ensure that the contributions of IARCs, CRSPs, and centrally and regionally funded activities are fully utilized in achieving Agency agricultural development objectives. Donor coordination can help to prevent the fragmentation of national programs that can result when diverse projects are put in place without considering redundancy and complementarities.

Cooperation for Development in Africa (CDA), an informal association of the seven major bilateral donors to Africa who provide 65 percent of direct development assistance, represents one organized effort of donors to cooperate. Within CDA, A.I.D., the largest donor to agricultural research systems, serves as the overall coordinator of assistance in agricultural research. A.I.D. and the World Bank have agreed to cooperate in exploring development of faculties of agriculture in Africa. A.I.D. is supporting World Bank initiatives to promote IARC–led commodity networks in Africa. A.I.D. also works through World Bank Consultative Group meetings, UNDP Round Table meetings, and other opportunities.

A.I.D. believes that, in the last analysis, donor cooperation will only be successful when host country governments take the lead in establishing coherent programs into which donor resources may be placed. Hence, A.I.D. will work with African colleagues and counterparts to establish strong national research strategies or plans, and seek to use them as the framework for coordinating donor assistance to research and faculties of agriculture.

In summary, A.I.D. support in Africa for agricultural research and faculties of agriculture will adhere to five guiding principles which are key to effective agricultural technology development in Africa.

1. **Explicit Program Objectices and Priorities.** We will focus the bulk of our resources on a relatively limited set of countries, commodities, and research problems (particularly on the relationship of soil and water to the key commodities) where sustained assistance is most likely to achieve high payoff in producing new technology and income streams for producers.

2. **Balanced and Integrated Commodity and Socio-Economic Research.** We will give increased attention to the development of strong commodity research programs, while refining the role of

farming systems research, to ensure that on-station research programs respond to the real concerns of African farmers. This includes renewed attention to the problems and potentials of commercialization of agriculture and to labor availability and utilization.

3. **Sustained and Stable Support for U.S. and International Institutions.** We will increase the capacity of several lead Title XII institutions to support A.I.D. country, commodity, and problem priorities. We will also encourage and assist IARCs to establish a stronger presence in the development of African national research systems as well as regional commodity networks.

4. **Long-Term Commitment.** We will adopt a period of 20 to 25 years as the minimal acceptable planning period for assistance to African agricultural research systems and faculties of agriculture, as well as our support for the U.S. and international institutions upon whose expertise we depend.

5. **Donor Cooperation.** We will continue to facilitate donor cooperation in African agricultural research and faculties of agriculture. Our efforts will have two emphases: effective collaboration among donors and development of long-term national agricultural research strategies or programs into which diverse donor resources can be effectively placed.

The implementation of these guiding principles will not guarantee the elimination of hunger in Africa. I believe, however, that with these efforts, the mass famine afflicting Africa today will not be repeated again and again.

The ultimate objectives of United States assistance in food and agriculture are to enable African countries to become self-reliant in food, assure food security, and achieve economic growth.

There is no certainty that these objectives can be achieved by African countries. However, there is certainty that the objectives will not be achieved unless fundamental efforts are initiated now.

Technology alone cannot do the entire job. Institutional innovations, policy supports, and infrastructure investments must occur if agriculture is to develop and benefits are to be spread widely among rural populations. However, without improved agricultural technologies, resulting from research, few development programs will move very far or have lasting effect.

From experience, we know how to go about developing the tools of technology; the incentive pricing policies; and the institutions. What is needed is the long-term commitment of African governments and donor nations. A green revolution for Africa can happen if the world works together to make it happen.

We know that food self-reliance is crucial for sustained economic productivity in Africa, but that is only part of the equation. I'd like to discuss briefly another kind of revolution. Side by side with the slowly evolving green revolution in Africa is the emergence of a complementary and rapidly growing phenomenon that holds the potential of great promise. Although I hesitate to overuse the term, it is, nonetheless, a 'revolution' of the entrepreneur.

A combination of factors, the crumbling of centralized planning schemes, rapid population growth and high unemployment have resulted in a tremendous number of small enterprises cropping up in many countries. Walking through a small town in the Delta in Egypt, or along the streets of Bamako, Mali, you see hundreds of little shops busily producing furniture, metal work, baskets, and a great variety of other items. This is not a big business revolution but a grassroots entrepreneurial revolution.

At A.I.D., we are seeking ways to conduct our development program so as to encourage the rising small scale entrepreneur who is moving to fill the economic vacuum left by failed statist policies. Here again, as in the Green Revolution, we need a policy climate conducive to growth.

In conclusion, I want to share with you a simple poem written by a farmer in Costa Rica, which appeared in the Newsletter of the Pan American Development Foundation. His feelings, I believe, reflect the feelings of small farmers everywhere.

> I am the one who comes to the city once in a while. . .
> I am the one who looks in awe at the city with an open mouth. . .
> I am the one who struggles from sunrise to sunrise to bring a better product to your table. . .
> I am the one who thinks everyone has turned their back to me. . .
> I am the one with calloused hands and a grieving spirit. . . yet with the hope of a better tomorrow.
> I don't know if my children will be able to continue their education; they walk barefoot and sometimes cry from hunger.
> My shack has a shattered roof, and my five children sleep in the same uncovered bed.
> But I dislike being called 'poor peasant'
> Even though I am a poor peasant.
> I have pride and I am deeply human. . . and can show that I am responsible. . .
> Just give me the opportunity and I shall produce. . .
> I shall produce a better tomorrow for my family and for my country.*

*Reprinted with permission of Pan American Development Foundation News—Winter 1985

M. Peter McPherson, a former Peace Corps volunteer, was appointed by President Reagan as administrator of the Aid for International Development in 1981. As administrator of AID, he oversees and directs U.S. economic development operations in more than 60 Third World countries. He is also chairman of the Board of the Overseas Private Investment Corporation, and has served on the Board of International Food and Agricultural Development. The American Lebanese League presented him with the "Humanitarian of the Year Award" in 1983.

# THE PHYSIOLOGY OF HUNGER AND MALNUTRITION

## Peter L. Pellett

## Table of Contents

# PROLOGUE

When used in describing the global food and nutrition situation, the words 'hunger' and 'starvation' both imply similar meanings. In other contexts, however, (Balagura 1973, Booth 1978) 'hunger' may refer to the control of feeding behavior and thus paradoxically can be used (eg Novin et al 1976) in relation to discussions on the etiology of obesity.

In English usage the words 'starve' and 'starvation' can have a gradation of meanings extending from mild hunger to death. The most apposite definitions of starvation from the Oxford English Dictionary are "To cause to perish of hunger; to deprive of or keep scantily supplied with food; to subdue by famine or low diet; and to produce atrophy by withholding nutriment." Using these definitions, the words hunger and starvation will be used to describe a wide range of conditions extending from levels of intake which are below 'adequacy' to absolute deprivation.

Since vitamins and minerals are involved in the actions of enzymes, a vast range of physiological and biochemical abnormalities exist as a result of mineral and vitamin deficiencies and are the subject of countless research papers. There is no doubt as to the world-wide importance of these deficiencies and the phenomena caused are certainly within the scope of a review on the physiology of hunger and malnutrition. This paper will, however, concentrate on deficiencies of energy and protein in the diet and will thus give major consideration to starvation, hunger and protein-energy malnutrition. Physiological changes can also affect psychology and behavior; these effects have also been widely discussed and researched (Keys et al 1950, Scrimshaw and Gordon 1968, Kallen 1973, Cravioto et al 1974, Olson 1975, Wershow 1975, Brozek 1982), but will not be discussed further in this review. In addition, water deprivation (Wolf 1958, Epstein et al 1973, Peters et al 1975, Rolls and Rolls 1982) will be excluded from consideration though, in the development of hunger and malnutrition especially in the drought-prone areas, its direct and indirect (Chen 1983) roles may be fundamental.

The use above of the word adequacy, raises another question in that such a concept must be defined. What is 'adequate' will vary amongst other factors, with the age, sex, activity pattern and previous health of the individual as well as with the diet itself. Adequacy can be defined both in relation to the food received as well as to the effect of that food on the consumer: problems can arise in interpretation with either (Pellett 1985).

Certainly one can appear pedantic in emphasizing definitions since acute hunger or starvation is recognisable to all; however, the consequences of long-term 'inadequate' intakes of food may be profound both for individuals and for societies. The reason for this is fundamental in that 'adaptation' to deficiency has evolved with the primary 'aim' of survival.

Further problems, as with the whole role of nutrition as a discipline, are that causes and solutions are rarely simple. Even the apparently simple cause and effect of drought leading to starvation must involve considerations of *inter alia* individual and national poverty, food distribution systems, population pressures, migration and the interactions of nutrition and disease. Some of the complexities are obvious in relation to the current famine in Africa and have been discussed concerning previous famines and/or severe food restrictions imposed by war (Burger *et al* 1984, Keys *et al* 1950, Dept. Exper. Med., 1951, Woodham–Smith, 1962, Blix *et al* 1971, Bang 1978, Cox 1978, Currey 1978, Dando 1983).

For the individual a series of events occurs as dietary intake diverges more and more from the habitual. If 'requirement' be used loosely to represent these habitual intakes, as deprivation proceeds, adaptation to the deprivation leads to new 'requirement' values such that eventually balance is obtained at these new lower levels. Adaptation can include both use of body stores and reduction of energy expenditure.

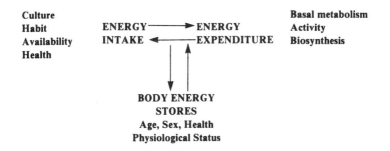

Obviously absolute deprivation leads eventually to death but at intermediate levels of intake survival may be possible for extremely long periods but at a high degree of social cost. This concept is especially relevant to energy balance; Bcaton (1983) indicates that in the widest sense all individuals and communities eventually adapt to reach 'energy balance' but whether this is at a level beneficial for the individual or society is a completely different consideration. The additional question must always be posed 'requirement for what?' (FAO/WHO/UNU/1985).

The sequence described in Fig. 1 illustrates the various stages that are involved as deprivation proceeds. While obvious starvation lies towards the bottom of the figure, problems may exist at any level of deprivation. In addition, the role of disease is fundamental since the symptoms of malnutrition and starvation arise, not only by the absence of food but also from secondary causes such as infection which reduce intake and/or absorption of the available food. If nutritional intake is less than the amount required to meet the continuing metabolic needs of the organism, a sequence of events is set in motion that leads, eventually, to the appearance of symptoms of clinical deficiency states. Initially, the content of the nutrient in body tissues and fluids falls. If the deficiency continues, biochemical and physiological lesions develop, such as reduced plasma albumin and a deficient level of enzymes necessary for the normal maintenance of cell function. These events may be considered to be characteristic of the subclinical phase of nutritional disease and they are followed eventually by the appearance of clinical signs and symptoms indicative of the nutrient deficiency.

## NUTRITION AT THE GLOBAL LEVEL

### Changing Concepts in Causation of Malnutrition

Major changes have taken place over the last two decades in the ways that malnutrition and its causation are viewed on a global basis. (Pellett 1983). Many reasons have contributed to these changes in perception, but a major one was the realization (e.g. Scrimshaw *et al* 1968) that malnutrition and infection bore a synergistic relation to each other. Further, it also became clear that solutions to the problem of malnutrition, to be successful, required more than simple provision of food and nutrients and that there was a causal relationship between malnutrition, poverty, and economic development. It is no coincidence that the victims of famine and starvation are always the poor and deprived. Health care facilities differ widely, usually also as a consequence of poverty. The WHO Sixth Report on The World Health Situation (1980) shows that the range between the best and worst infant mortality rates (of which nutrition can be a major causative feature) can differ by a factor of 25:1 (from a high of 200 to a low of 8 infant deaths for every 1000 births) and, even more dramatically, maternal mortality may differ by a factory of 200 to 1 (from a high of 1000 to a low of 5 deaths per 100,000 population).

Over the last few decades, the traditional deficiency diseases such as scurvy, beri–beri and pellagra, have declined in prevalence but, in contrast, protein–energy malnutrition in children is still increasing, especially in the urban slums of developing countries. However, estimates of those suffering from hunger and malnutrition have differed widely, and have fallen to less than 20% of the world's population (FAO 1980), from a high of more than 60% about twenty years ago.

The nutrition situation has not improved to this extent although there are some positive trends for some regions of the world. Africa, however, remains the region with the most problems and least progress

(Eicher 1982, Sai 1984) and has shown a decline in per capita food availability in recent years (FAO 1983). This may be a consequence of the very rapid population growth in the continent (Sai 1984) with its impact on deforestation, erosion, and climatic change (Brown 1981, Biswas and Biswas 1979).

The major reason for the discrepancy between the more recent and the earlier estimates is that different assumptions were used in assessing the numbers malnourished with the more recent estimates being far more stringent. All were obtained from Food Balance Sheet data for protein and/or calorie availability compared to 'requirements'. Difficulties have arisen in defining requirements (Beaton 1983, FAO/WHO/UNU 1985) especially when the process of adaptation is considered. It has been suggested that the efficiency of energy utilization may vary significantly even in the same individual at different levels of intake (Sukhatme and Margen 1982). This hypothesis, however, remains unproven (Garrow and Blaza 1982) and is disputed by Rand and Scrimshaw (1984). The more recent estimates (FAO 1977) no longer attempt to define energy requirements as such but consider that intakes below $1.2 \times BMR$ are reaching the critical limit (Alamgir 1980) 'below which the individual's ability to carry out minimum necessary activity would be seriously impaired'. Irrespective of the actual numbers involved, hunger and malnutrition remain problems of massive proportions and are major contributory factors to reduced life expectancy in developing countries (Table 1).

**Food and Nutrients**

More than 40 separate elements or compounds have now been identified as necessary for life. While all these materials are required for daily metabolism to proceed it is not necessary that they all be provided daily in the diet. The ability of the body to draw on reserves or stores allows varying times to elapse before deficiencies may be recognised. Oxygen (if that be a nutrient) is needed almost continuously, water deprivation cannot last for more than a few days, total food deprivation can last for weeks to months depending on fat reserves while for Vitamin A the stores may be adequate to last for more than a year on essentially zero intake. Daily requirements for nutrients also vary enormously ranging from microgram quantities for Vitamin $B_{12}$, milligram quantities for many minerals and most vitamins, gram quantities for individual amino acids, calcium and phosphorus and several hundred gram quantities of energy providing materials.

Other than in extreme circumstances, the ability to blame to a diet in the development of malnutrition is much less direct than many assume. Nutritional status and health status overlap; adaptation to high or low

41

intakes may occur; nutritional requirements, while based on scientific facts, depend on informed judgments and are subject to a wide range of individual variability; and finally estimates of nutrient intakes are only approximate except under controlled metabolic conditions which are hardly normal.

TABLE 1

PREVALENCE OF UNDERNUTRITION AND LIFE EXPECTANCY
IN DEVELOPING REGIONS OF THE WORLD
(Source: FAO 1982)

| Region | No. of Countries | Undernourished Millions | % of Pop. | Life Expectancy at Birth (yrs.)* |
|--------|------------------|-------------------------|-----------|----------------------------------|
| Africa | 37 | 72 | 20 | 49 |
| Latin America | 24 | 41 | 11 | 65 |
| Near East | 14 | 19 | 9 | 56 |
| Far East | 15 | 303 | 23 | 56 |
| Total | 90 | 436 | 19 | 56 |

*For developed countries Life Expectancy is 70-74 years (WHO 1980a).

While the term malnutrition should strictly include overnutrition and some of the diseases of affluence, it will be used here to mean only the condition resulting from a deficient intake of energy or of a particular nutrient. Four especially important and broad causes of hunger and malnutrition are:an insufficient supply of the foods necessary for a balanced diet, often due to agricultural failure but also due to poverty; an uneven distribution of the available food (both between and within families); a lack of knowledge about food, nutrition and health; and infectious diseases which are synergistic to malnutrition (Latham, 1979).

It is now realized that malnutrition may frequently be caused less by nutrient deficiency (as such) and more by many interrelated social, political and economic factors; the widespread prevalency of hunger and malnutrition is usually a symptom of a very sick society (Maletnlema, 1980). Because of this multifactorial causation, solutions must also be multifaceted, even if concepts such as the elimination of poverty and improvement of living standards are basic. Malnutrition affects the growth, development and survival of children as well as the health, activity and well–being of adults. Conventional solutions in the form of specific programs are usually inadequate to tackle problems, and their effects are transitory since they do not reach causes. Nutrition can be improved through upgrading the level of living—particularly of real income, food availability and health services. Thus, solutions lie mostly outside the traditional nutritional field but are brought about through economic and social development. (Mason *et al* 1984).

## Major Nutritional Disorders

The characteristics of the major world nutritional disorders are summarized in Table 2 and the fundamental role of causative factors in the areas of health, wealth and sanitation must be recognized. Nevertheless, depending on the disorder, actions can be taken to improve the nutritional status of the most vulnerable groups which are women of childbearing age and young children.

Problems other than these, such as scurvy, rickets, beri-beri, and pellagra still exist but are generally less widespread than those conditions tabulated. Hunger is widespread and ranges from the gross manifestation of prolonged starvation to mild and apparently reversible growth failure. Protein-energy malnutrition and the factors causing low birth weight in babies overlap to a considerable degree with hunger (WHO 1980b, UNICEF, 1984), so much so that they may become indistinguishable. The majority of low birth weight infants ( 2500 g) in developing countries are those of normal gestational age. The frequency of birth of these infants is more than twice as great as in developed countries (WHO, 1980b; UNICEF, 1984). Such children are more prone to infections and also lag behind in their subsequent development (Mata and Behar 1975, Omalulu *et al,* 1981). This increased prevalence can have significant social cost (Griffey-Brechin 1984). Maternal dietary supplements can increase birth weight (Lechtig *et al,* 1979), but in environments where health care is frequently lacking the potential for maternal mortality is unfortunately high (WHO 1980a). Furthermore, the desire by mothers for small babies (and easier birth) should be recognized since this can negate programs for nutrition intervention until health care facilities are improved.

The world prevalence of protein-energy malnutrition (P-EM) has been estimated using data from a number of large scale surveys (Bengoa 1973, Bengoa and Donoso, 1974; Puffer and Serrano, 1973), it is probable that some 90 million cases of protein-energy malnutrition of varying severity currently exist in the developing regions. These numbers probably represent a minimum since many children are reported to have died from infectious disease where malnutrition was a likely underlying or a major, simultaneous cause. Procedures for the rehabilitation of the severely malnourished child have been recently reviewed by Solomons (1985).

Another nutritional problem of considerable significance is hypovitaminosis A, considered to be the most common cause of blindness in the developing areas of the world (WHO, 1976; Underwood, 1978, McKigney 1985). Recent estimates (Sommer *et al,* 1982) from studies in rural

TABLE 2

THE CHARACTERISTICS OF HUNGER AND THE MAJOR NUTRITIONAL DISORDERS[1]

| | Hunger[a] | Protein energy malnutrition (PEM[b]) | | Xeropthalmia | Goitre | Iron deficiency anaemia | Low birth weight infants |
|---|---|---|---|---|---|---|---|
| | | Nutritional marasmus | Kwashiorkor | | | | |
| Causation/ precipitation Long term | Poverty, poor agriculture | | Low protien diet | Low intakes of carotene and/or retinol | Low intakes of iodine | Low intake/absorption of iron | Poor dietary intake since conception. Infections of mother |
| Immediate | Poverty, crop failure, war | Early weaning; infections | Infections | Early weaning; infections | | Blood loss from infections | Low weight gain in pregnancy |
| Vulnerable groups and main age of incidence | All ages | Children less than one year | Children between 1-2 years | Children, preschool | Older children females | Children (under 3) and females of children bearing age | Mothers of poor socio-economic status |

| | Major features | Consequences |
|---|---|---|
| | Growth failure, wasting, lethargy | Reduced growth, reduced work capacity, high mortality |
| | Wasting | High mortality, impaired mental development |
| | Oedema, fatty liver, reduced serum albumin | High mortality, impaired mental development |
| | Night blindness, xerosis of conjunctive and cornea, keratomalacia, low serum retinol | High mortality especially when associated with PEM Blindness |
| | Enlarged thyroid | Cretinism |
| | Low Haemoglobin (microcytic hypochronic anaemia, if severe) | Pallor, reduced work and learning efficiency |
| | Hypoglycemia, hypothermia, poor resistance to infection (low IgC) | High mortality, sub-optimal development. High incidence of infection |

[1] With acknowledgements to D.S. McLaren, Ed., Community Nutrition J. Wiley and Sons 1973.

[a] There is a considerable degree of overlap with PEM and LBW infants.

[b] PEM when early or of mild-moderate severity is usually sub-clinical and can only be diagnosed by anthropometric criteria (Wt/age and Wt/Ht).

[c] Infants of birth weight below 2,500 g. In developing countries the majority of these are due to fetal growth retardation.

Indonesia indicate a rate of 2.7 per 1000 for corneal xerophthalmia amongst the pre-school population. Half of these cases probably develop bilateral blindness. Extrapolation of this rate to the combined pre-school populations of Bangladesh, India, Indonesia and the Philippines would indicate 500,000 cases per year of corneal xerophthalmia with up to ten times as many less severe (e.g. Bitots spots) cases.

It seems likely that hypovitaminosis A, as a public health problem, will only be eliminated when the society has access to a diet sufficient in vitamin A and also in the other nutrients that affect vitamin A metabolism. This, however, requires a generally more equitable distribution of the benefits of national development. Serious hypovitaminosis A occurs most frequently in countries where protein-energy malnutrition of children and generalized poverty are also major problems (Underwood, 1978).

## Assessment of Nutritional Status

Techniques for the evaluation of the nutritional status of populations can be separated into two major categories, the first pertaining to agriculture and food availability, the second pertaining to health and vital statistics.

Agriculture and food production data (FAO 1980) have limitations, but they can indicate approximate availability of food supplies and nutrients to a population. Close examination of agricultural production data can also allow judgments on the success or failure of agricultural techniques. The next level of information concerning food derives from dietary surveys and food consumption patterns within the society and provides data upon socio-economic variables and the distribution and storage of foods. Dietary surveys are difficult to perform with accuracy, but can give the most detailed information of food and nutrient consumption at the family level. Conversion of food intake to nutrient intake is now performed rapidly using computers, but is still dependent on both judgment and the accuracy of food-table data.

Once nutrient intake data are established, these must be compared with standards before decisions can be made concerning the nutritional value of the diet. Derivation of the appropriate requirement standards and comparison with intake values do not always allow clearcut conclusions concerning either the nutrient levels or the diet as a whole. The essential component of most definitions of nutrient requirement or recommended allowances is the concept that they refer to needs of nutrients to maintain health in already healthy individuals. Amongst normal individuals, requirements of many nutrients are affected by the nature of the diet, body size, activity, age, sex and physiological state. The recommended dietary allowance is considered to take into account individual variability and to meet the requirements of almost all individuals in a group of specified characteristics. For food energy, in contrast, average requirements are specified because there may be a risk to health from either inadequate or excess intake of sources of energy.

Human protein and energy needs are addressed in depth about every decade by international groups (FAO 1957ab, FAO/WHO 1965, 1973), under the auspices of the Food and Agricultural Organization (FAO) and the World Health Organization (WHO). For the most recent discussions in 1981-1982, the United Nations University (UNU) also collaborated. While actual recommended allowances for protein and energy will not differ greatly from previous recommendations, the basis used for both recommendations has changed. For energy, the new report notes the apparent paradox of the survival of populations consuming only 80 percent of their estimated energy needs. These populations adapt to these lower energy intakes by reduction in activity. This has been documented by Viteri (1976) for Guatemalan plantation workers who are limited by their food intake in their work productive capacity and remain almost inactive for the remainder of the day. When additional food is provided, both consumption and activity increase. The new report then emphasizes the importance of adequate food for discretionary as well as work activities and underlines the obvious (but often ignored) concept that there is no appropriate average figure for energy requirement unless the activity level is also specified. Not only do individuals adapt, but whole societies may develop patterns compatible with low food intake which may not, however, be compatible with their long-term interest.

The FAO/WHO/UNU group throughout their report ask the question—requirement for what? Thus, it is suggested that energy requirements should be specified for a pattern of work and discretionary activities appropriate to the various populations and subpopulations concerned. A simplified approach for estimates of energy needs has been suggested where needs are defined as: Food Energy Need = Basal Needs × Activity (as a factor). Basal Needs are calculated from a formula (e.g. Harris and Benedict 1919, FAO/WHO/UNU 1985), which includes sex, age and weight; activity factors are either calculated from daily activity patterns or an appropriate factor is assigned. These assigned factors (per 24 hours) would range from 1.4 for light activity to 2.2 for heavy activity. The factor of 1.2 used to assess the number malnourished in the world (FAO 1977, 1981) is obviously very low and it is assumed that below the level of intake which this represents, normal acitvity is no longer possible.

For protein, it has been recognized for some years that the safe daily allowance of 0.57g/Kg of high quality protein (egg, fish, milk), recommended by the FAO/WHO (1973) Committee was too low (Garza et al, 1977). The FAO/ WHO/UNU (1985) Committee reviewed a number of short (weeks) and long-term (months) protein requirement studies in humans and concluded that the new safe protein allowance should be 0.75 g/Kg, again expressed as egg, fish or milk. This is an apparent increase of 30%. Recommended allowances will increase far less than this, because previously there had been an excessively large correction factor for protein quality. In practice values for the adult will be almost unchanged. A selection of some of the new international protein allowances are shown in Table 3.

TABLE 3

SAFE LEVELS OF PROTEIN INTAKE (gm protein/kg body wt.*)
As proposed by FAO/WHO/UNU (1985).

| Age Group | Males | | Females |
|---|---|---|---|
| 3-6 months | | 1.85 | |
| 6-9 months | | 1.65 | |
| 9-12 months | | 1.5 | |
| 1-2 years | | 1.2 | |
| 2-3 years | | 1.15 | |
| 3-5 years | | 1.1 | |
| 5-12 years | | 1.0 | |
| 12-14 years | 1.0 | | 0.95 |
| 14-16 years | 1.0 | | 0.9 |
| 16-18 years | 0.95 | | 0.8 |
| Adults | 0.75 | | 0.75 |
| Pregnancy | | | + 6 gm** |
| Lactation 0-6 mo. | | | + 17.5 gm** |
| 6 mo.+ | | | + 13 gm** |

* Uncorrected for biological values (amino acid scores) of mixed dietary proteins for infants and children and for digestibility for all groups.
** Total daily addition per subject.

The background to the new estimates (FAO/WHO/UNU 1985) is that even in the steady state, body proteins constantly undergo breakdown and resynthesis. When growth is occurring, not only is there a net deposition of protein, but the rates of both synthesis and breakdown are increased. The principles underlying this process of protein turnover now have been described in some detail (e.g. see Waterlow *et al,* 1978).

Briefly, the rates of protein turnover vary from tissue to tissue, and the relative contributions of different tissues to total protein turnover in the body change with age and adaptation to various levels of protein intake (see Waterlow *et al,* 1978; Young and Pellett 1983, Young *et al,* 1984). The amino acids released by breakdown are reused for protein synthesis but this process of reutilization is not completely efficient. Some amino acids are lost by oxidative catabolism, and for this reason, both essential amino acids and a dietary source of utilizable nitrogen are needed.

The daily turnover of body proteins is, in fact, several-fold greater than the total intake of protein, showing that the reutilization of amino acids is a major contributory factor to the economy of body protein metabolism (Young and Scrimshaw, 1978). In essence, therefore, the protein requirement is determined initially by the amount of nitrogen and amino acids that must be supplied to meet the continued loss of amino acids, due to their incomplete reutilization. This cycle of amino acid and protein metabolism is depicted in Figure 2. Protein requirement in practice comprises the two major components of protein quantity and protein quality (Pellett and Young 1980), and the two concepts are inclusive in the final numerical value specified for daily requirements. Amino acid needs are now known in more detail for all ages (FAO/WHO/UNU 1985) and have been suggested as a basis for designing supplementary food mixtures for infant feeding (Young and Pellett 1984).

Observations on the health of populations are also used to indicate nutritional status although impairment of health can only be directly ascribed to faulty nutrition when corresponding food and nutrient intake data are available to correlate with the health data. These data start at the regional or county level by using vital and health statistics and can identify the extent of risk to the community. For the individual, nutritional assessment includes anthropometric, biochemical and clinical studies. Consideration of the results of such surveys can give information on the effects of nutrition on physical development, on the impairment of biochemical function and on the deviation from health due to malnutrition. Assessment of nutritional status by newer functional tests (Solomon and Allen, 1983) may allow more specific conclusions to be drawn concerning nutrient deficiency and health when the deficiency is marginal.

Poor apparent nutritional status, as measured by inadequate growth and development of children, may of course be more related to infective disease, water supply and sanitation than directly to food availability and food selection and is further complicated by the synergistic relationship between them. Even the type of measurement used can allow varying conclusions to be drawn (Table 4). Weight-for-age in children may overestimate the prevalence of malnutrition to a considerable degree when compared to weight-for-height measurements. Children from poor environments may weigh less than well-nourished children of the same age but have, however, become adapted to the situation and may be apparently healthy. Are these children suffering from hunger and malnutrition or not? The answer is dependent on the definition used or perhaps on the use of more detailed tests which can refine the term "apparently healthy".

TABLE 4

COMPARISON BETWEEN NUMBERS OF CHILDREN ASSESSED
AS MALNOURISHED USING VARIOUS ANTHROPOMETRIC CRITERIA
IN THE NATIONAL NUTRITION SURVEY OF EGYPT (AID 1978)

| | Percentages assessed as Malnourished and Anthropometric Criteria Used for Assessment | | |
|---|---|---|---|
| Diagnosis | Weight for Height | Weight for Age | Weight for Age |
| Normal | 95% | 78% | 53% |
| Moderately Malnourished | 2% | 17% | 38% |
| Severely Malnourished | less than 1% | 5% | 9% |

Note:  There were 8016 (4240 males and 3776 females) children below the age of 6
years. Normal was defined as above 85% of the reference standard
population for Wt/Ht and above 90% for Ht/Age and Wt/Age. Moderately
malnourished was between 80-84. 9% Wt/Ht, 85-89.9% Ht/Age and 75-
89.9% Wt/Age. Severely malnourished was defined as less than 80% Wt/Ht,
less than 85% Ht/Age and less than 75% Wt/Age. The latter category thus
includes Gomez 2nd degree and 3rd degree malnutrition.

## STARVATION AND MALNUTRITION

### Historical Background

The history of studies in starvation and famine was extensively
reviewed by Keys et al (1950). More recent reviews include Woodham-
Smith (1962), Blix et al (1978), Cox (1978), and Dando (1983), with the
latter review drawing present day insights from Biblical famines. Some of
the early experimental studies involved the use of professional fasters
which, as Garrow (1974) remarks, make fascinating reading but lead to
equivocal conclusions since such individuals are hardly normal. At the
beginning of the century Benedict and his associates conducted some not-
able experiments (Benedict 1907, 1915, Benedict et al (1919) which are still
relevant today. With the tremendous amount of starvation unleashed by
World War II (see Burger et al 1948, Keys et al 1950, Dept. Expt. Medicine 1951), the monumental study of Keys et al (1950) on 32 volunteer
conscientious objectors was undertaken, from which a great deal of our
present knowledge is derived. Any serious student of these problems is
urged to read the two extensive volumes published in 1950. It is probable
with our present human experimentation regulations that no such studies

could now be undertaken—a cynic might remark that despite this, we still allow more drastic natural experiments to occur on other continents.

Following the introduction of total fasting in the treatment of obesity (Bloom 1959, Duncan *et al* 1962) many studies have been performed on experimental subjects and the biochemical background has become much clearer (Aoki *et al* 1975, Cahill *et al* 1966, Felig *et al* 1969, 1971, Flatt and Blackburn 1974, Owen *et al* 1969, 1978, 1979). Valuable reviews on the metabolic and physiological responses to starvation are by Kleiber (1961), Cahill (1970, 1978) Young and Scrimshaw (1971), Blackburn and Phinney (1983) and Levenson and Seifter (1983). It should be emphasized here that the majority of detailed biochemical investigations into starvation have been upon obese subjects since starvation in these circumstances can be viewed as therapeutic not experimental. The extension of these results to subjects without large fat reserves should be performed with caution.

### Body Weights, Organ Weights, and Body Composition

The enormous early literature on famine, natural and experimental starvation and their effects on the size and appearance of organs and tissues of the body has been reviewed by Keys and his associates in their two volume 'magnum opus' on human starvation (Keys *et al* 1950).

Weight varies to a large degree in well fed individuals and in famine situations no data are generally available on the pre-starvation weights. This often makes interpretation of early data difficult. Porter (1889), for example, reported on autopsy observations of the Madras famine of 1877, but no pre-famine weights were available. Subsequent estimates of the weight loss have been made, however, using known weights for a similar population in India. An autopsy on 30 subjects without edema, indicated about 28% of original body weight had probably been lost or some 14.5 Kg. Another 13 men who showed famine edema had no significant weight loss, however, and Keys *et al* 1950 remark that "the percentage loss of gross weight was negligible and by no means represented the serious disturbance of the nutritional status of these patients". The causation of the edema of famine, (ie relative increases in the extracellular water) remains obscure. A major problem is that it does not always occur despite the level of deprivation and other conditions being apparently similar. Edema in Kwashiorkor is perhaps more easily explained, although there are still a number of anomalies (Coward and Lunn 1981).

Data from World War II prison camps show losses of 22% body weight in Singapore and as much as 40% in German concentration camps (Keys *et al* 1950). Levenson and Seifter (1983) claim that most previously healthy adults can tolerate a weight loss of 5–10% with relatively little functional disorganization. At the other extreme, save for exceptional individuals, human beings and animals do not survive weight losses greater than 40%. Fluctuations in, and the degree of, edema can, however, mask overall weight changes.

During a controlled experiment in Minnesota on starvation (Keys *et al* 1950), some 24% average weight loss was produced over a period of 24 weeks by feeding diets approximating 1550 Kcal/day compared to previous intakes of more than 3000 Kcal/day. This loss was similar to that found in natural famine, but without the superimposed stresses of deprivation and disease. In the rehabilitation phase some degree of over-compensation occurred and between 20 and 33 weeks of rehabilitation the weights of subjects averaged 9% above control values. When edema is present, weight loss can occur in the early stages of a refeeding: this also occurs in Kwashiorkor. In the Minnesota experiment, six of the 32 subjects showed small weight losses in the first week of refeeding. The mean weight gain after six weeks refeeding remained small and it took ten weeks of refeeding before all subjects registered weight gains.

Wasting of the tissue is a characteristic feature of starvation—the skin is loose, body fat declines, and there is marked atrophy of the skeletal muscles. This is also seen in marasmus of the child. In 359 autopsies on adults who died on 'pure' starvation in the Warsaw Ghetto, well preserved skeletal muscles were seen in less than 3% of subjects and severe atrophy was recorded for more than 60% (Stein and Fenigstein 1946). Other muscles respond in a similar manner and Indian famine victims examined by Porter (1889) showed extreme atrophy of all layers of the intestinal wall including the muscularis.

Other organs also show atrophy and many data have been tabulated by Keys *et al* (1950), from measurements on victims of World War II. Data from autopsies performed on subjects who died in the Warsaw ghetto show large losses of the liver and spleen (approaching 50%) but full conservation of the brain. In experimental starvation major alterations take place in the compartments of the body as is illustrated in Table 5. Important changes are the increases in extracellular fluid (SCN space), losses in fat but the maintenance of bone mineral. The fluid increases may in some cases be manifested as edema. Rehabilitation is also of interest and at 33 weeks of refeeding the 'overshoot' in body fat (as was earlier noted for body weight) is noteworthy. Although not shown in Table 5, by 58 weeks of rehabilitation mean body composition had returned close to control values.

Changes in body composition are reflections of tissue lost during deprivation. The rate of loss of protein, water, fat and of body weight is clearly dependent on the degree of deprivation and the length of time for which it was experienced. In the Minnesota experiment the loss of approximately 25% body weight, 41% muscle mass, and 68% fat was

## TABLE 5

### MINNESOTA EXPERIMENT ON CHANGES IN WEIGHTS AND PROPORTIONS FOR THE BODY COMPARTMENTS IN 32 SUBJECTS DURING 24 WEEKS OF STARVATION AND 33 WEEKS OF REHABILITATION

| Compart-ment | Control | | 12 Weeks Starvation | | 24 Weeks Starvation | | 33 Weeks Rehabilitation | |
|---|---|---|---|---|---|---|---|---|
| | Kg | % | Kg | % | Kg | % | Kg | % |
| Body Weight | 69.5 | 100.0 | 56.9 | 100.0 | 53.6 | 100.0 | 72.5 | 100.0 |
| Bone Mineral | 2.8 | 4.0 | 2.8 | 4.9 | 2.8 | 5.3 | 2.8 | 3.8 |
| Plasma | 3.2 | 4.5 | 3.2 | 5.6 | 3.4 | 6.5 | 3.0 | 4.2 |
| Red Cells | 2.7 | 3.9 | 2.1 | 3.7 | 2.0 | 3.8 | 2.6 | 3.5 |
| 'SCN' | 17.1 | 23.5 | 17.2 | 30.3 | 17.9 | 34.0 | 17.5 | 24.2 |
| Fat | 9.7 | 13.9 | 5.0 | 8.7 | 2.8 | 5.2 | 14.3 | 19.7 |
| 'Active' Tissue | 39.9 | 57.5 | 32.0 | 56.2 | 29.2 | 55.5 | 37.9 | 52.3 |

Active tissue is calculated as the total body weight less the sum of fat, bone mineral and thiocyanate space. Fat was calculated by underwater weighing. Extracellular fluid space was determined from the thiocyanate concentrations and was determined in the mornings, 12-16 hours post-prandial.

Source:  Keys et al (1950)

obtained by a six month (24 week) period approximating 50% of the normal food calorie intake.

Additional factors reflecting adaptation to starvation are discussed by Levenson and Seifter (1987). These include reductions in cardiac work and in the energy involved in muscle substrate uptake—a consequence of the biochemical adaptations discussed later, and changes in the proportions of red and white muscle fibers. The GI tract is also substantially changed with flattening of villi and a reduction in absorptive surface area; this is often accompanied by reduced disaccaridase activity. Liver can lose considerable amounts of weight but liver function frequently remains normal. The kidney appears to lose less weight than the liver (up to 25%) but will also maintain function for a long time in starvation.

**Work and Metabolic Rate**

Two important adaptations to starvation are reductions in activity and reductions in basal metabolic rate (BMR). The former is sometimes termed voluntary and the second involuntary. It is questionable how much reduction in physical activity can truly be called voluntary when inertia and lethargy are themselves sequellae of starvation. There are many social implications of food deprivation and the triad of problems: starvation, social disruption and disease (Foege 1971, Bang 1978) accompany all famines. The effects depend on the degree of deprivation experienced. Subjective estimates from a variety of sources by Keys *et al* (1950) show that both work performance and work capacity progressively fall in parallel with weight loss but that the potential for civil disorder and strife probably peak at about a 15–20% weight loss. Beyond this point and up to 50% weight loss, inertia and mental deterioration presumably increase such that lethargy predominates. In the final stage when body weight is one–half of normal, the subject is no longer capable of any physical work. Short periods of deprivation, however, can still allow marked physical activity. Cahill (1978) cites a marathon runner whose pre–race preparation was total calorie abstention for one week.

Changes in basal and/or resting metabolic rates as a result of starvation or undernutrition occur and are certainly involuntary adaptive mechanisms. There is a vast amount of early literature which has been comprehensively reviewed by Keys *et al* (1950). In two major experimental studies involving volunteers, the first by Benedict *et al* (1919) achieved a weight loss of approximately 10%, while the second by Keys *et al* (1950) produced a 25% weight loss. These studies have been critically reviewed by Garrow (1974).

In the study by Benedict *et al* (1919) performed in Springfield, Massachusetts, 34 subjects were fed diets aimed to produce approximately the 10 per cent loss in weight over 60 days. Normal levels of intake were about 3100 Kcal/day but were reduced to 2100 Kcal and then to 1500 Kcal/day. The experiment was performed in the fall of 1917 and there were two breaks, one for Thanksgiving and the other for Christmas. These breaks, which at first sight might have appeared to fatally flaw the experiment, in fact produced some of the more interesting findings. As the weight fell there were parallel decreases in BMR and in pulse rate. A four day break was allowed for Thanksgiving when the subjects were allowed to eat again ad–libitum. This short period of relaxation produced rapid increases in metabolic rate almost to normal levels which was not accompanied by any increase in mean body weight. A similar, but longer, break of two weeks was allowed over the Christmas–New Year period and in this period, though there was a 2 Kg increase in body weight (ca. 3%), BMR increased by some 20% to almost normal values. When dietary restriction was again enforced the BMR fell rapidly to the pre–Christmas values.

To quote Garrow (1974) directly—three points were established about the effect of undernutrition on metabolic rate: "first, that basal metabolic rate decreases during undernutrition to a greater extent than mere loss of body weight can explain; second, that the temporary refeeding can restore basal metabolism to normal levels before normal weight is restored; and third, that after temporary refeeding the metabolic rate falls more rapidly with food deprivation than it would in a well-fed subject."

In the Minnesota study (Keys *et al* 1950) the restriction was both longer and more severe. In this experiment BMR was reduced by 39% when 24% of body weight was lost, and BMR was also shown to decline in both per unit weight and in unit surface area terms. Refeeding following the 24 weeks of semi–starvation was not *ad libitum* as in the Benedict experiment but involved four subgroups whose food energy increments ranged from approximately 400 Kcal/day to 1600 Kcal/day. The mean for all was about 900 Kcal/day. In 12 days of refeeding these produced mean gains of BMR of some 20% with only an average 8% gain in body weight. In Table 6, a comparison is shown between the two experiments. Similar results were obtained in both experiments in that BMR declined with continued restricted intakes but there were increases following refeeding at levels well beyond the increases in body mass. Because of the different experimental design no rapid fall in BMR following the re–imposition of restriction could be observed in the Minnesota experiment.

The decrease in BMR is the sum of two effects: 1) the reduction in tissue mass and 2) the reduction in metabolic activity of that tissue. In both experiments it can be concluded that some 60–65% is due to the former and 35–40% due to the latter. The proportion of these two effects will, however, depend on the severity and extent of the restriction suffered. In severe chronic malnutrition tissue loss can be extreme but the metabolic rate per unit tissue is surprisingly normal (Garrow 1974). Data with malnourished children are more difficult to interpret since not only is there restricted growth but changes in body composition. The latter may be direct effects of the malnutrition and/or abnormal composition as a result of delayed maturation. With children the metabolic rate of a malnourished child is dependent on the current rate of growth (Brooke and Ashworth 1972) and is reduced in marasmus as a consequence of reductions in plasma thyroid hormones (Alleyne *et al* 1977). Garrow (1974) draws the conclusion that the factor which mainly determines the resting metabolic rate is the rate of protein synthesis.

TABLE 6

COMPARISON OF DATA OBTAINED IN TWO MAJOR
EXPERIMENTS ON CHANGES IN BMR
ON DEPRIVATION AND REFEEDING

|  | Benedict et al (1919) | Keys et al (1950) |
|---|---|---|
| No of Subjects | 34 | 32 |
| Days of Deprivation | 102 | 170 |
| Mean loss in Body Weight | -11% | -24% |
| Mean loss in BMR | -19% | -39% |
| **Refeeding** | | |
| Mean Gain in Body Weight | +3% | +8% |
| Mean Gain in BMR | +18% | +20% |

In the Benedict et al (1919) experiment refeeding was ad libitum for 18 days; in the Keys et al (1950) experiment the results are reported for 12 days refeeding with an average increment of about 900 Kcal/day over the semi-starvation diet. Refeeding gains are expressed in relation to the semi-starvation levels. Losses are expressed in relation to control values.

The adaptations experienced may be different when growth is occurring. Questions immediately arise as to which is affected first, activity or growth and how much would reduced activity affect behavioral development? These are important issues in the social effects of malnutrition and hunger (Brozek 1982). Similar and equally complex relationships can occur in pregnancy with the subsequent prevalence of low birthweight babies in socially deprived environments (WHO 1980b). Lactation

(Whitehead 1983) may also be affected, as are some of the inter-relationships between maternal diet, (Sampson and Jansen 1984), breast milk production and the return of fertility during lactation. These have major implications to maternal and child health and affect both infant nutrition and birth spacing. Again it is obvious that the adaptations to restricted intakes and the priorities that ensue are dependent not only on the severity of the dietary restriction, but also on the age, sex and physiological status of the individual concerned.

## Hormonal Changes

Almost all hormones are involved in the adaptations to food deprivation. Major changes occur in insulin, glucagon, growth hormone, catecholamines, thyroid hormones and antidiuretic hormone and these changes are reflected in alterations in carbohydrate, protein, fat, water and electrolyte metabolism (Cahill 1970, Alleyne et al 1972, Truswell 1975, Levenson and Seifer 1983). The major control of the hormonal changes is the early fall in blood glucose (Aoki et al 1975). This initiates the metabolic adaptations which attempt to maintain glucose homeostasis by changing utilization rates of the various energy stores. Insulin, glucagon, growth hormone and catecholamines are all involved in these early adaptations but changes in the ratios of insulin and glucagon produce the majority of the biochemical changes (Marliss et al 1970). The literature reveals considerable contradictions in reported levels of growth hormone, thyroid hormones, glucocorticoids and the catecholamines as a result of various degrees of malnutrition (Hansen 1975, Alleyne et al 1977) and/or starvation (Levenson and Seifter 1983). Important additional variables are the effects of infection, infestation, stress, disease and previous nutritional state. These hormonal changes are the result, not the cause, of malnutrition. The use of hormone products pushed by unscrupulous drug companies in some countries for the home treatment of malnutrition can be actively harmful and should be condemned vigorously.

## Biochemical Changes

Since survival is paramount, all responses to starvation involve biochemical and physiological adaptations to ensure survival for as long as possible. A key to understanding the 'rationale' behind the various adaptations necessary can be seen from body composition (Table 7). The major variable is fat; carbohydrate stores, as glycogen, are minimal. Since fat cannot be converted to glucose in any significant amount the majority of the adaptations to acute starvation involve the continued provision of energy to organs such as nervous tissue that are normally completely dependent on glucose. Carbohydrate stores would be exhausted in one day or less of starvation while fat and protein stores for a normal individual at a low activity level could last for months. For individuals with large fat reserves survival would be much longer. For the obese individual in Table 7, the stores of approximately 37 Kg of fat, at an expenditure of 1600 Kcal/day, would allow some 200 days of survival. Total starvation for a year may indeed be possible for very obese subjects (Cahill 1978). Survival times would be reduced if higher physical activity were required, if the environment were cold and insulation was minimal, and if fat reserves were small.

TABLE 7

BODY COMPOSITION IN OVER AND UNDER NUTRITION

|  | Obese | Normal | Starvation | Stores Available (1) | Daily Utilization (2) |
|  | ............. Kg ................... |  |  | ............. grams ........... |  |
| --- | --- | --- | --- | --- | --- |
| Protein | 12.0 | 11.5 | 8.5 | 3,000 | 30(3) |
| Fat | 40.0 | 9.0 | 2.5 | 6,500 | 150 |
| Carbohydrate | 0.5 | 0.5 | 0.3 | 150 | 150 |
| Water | 44.5 | 40.0 | 34.0 |  |  |
| Minerals | 4.0 | 4.0 | 3.5 |  |  |
| Total | 101.0 | 65.0 | 48.8 |  |  |

(1) Assumes normal available store for 65 Kg man.
(2) Assumes expenditure of ca. 1500 Kcal/day for 65 Kg man.
(3) Represents an average throughout, although protein utilization may be 75 g/day at the beginning and 20 g/day in prolonged starvation.
Adapted from data of Passmore and Durnin (1967).

For a full understanding of the biochemistry of deprivation both the integration of metabolic pathways and the storage pattern of nutrients must be briefly considered. All the major dietary components-carbohydrates, proteins or fats can be used in the mitochondria of cells as energy by being converted through various routes into Acetyl–coenzyme A (Acetyl CoA) (Fig 3). Conversely these same materials can be synthesized by the body from biochemical intermediaries derived originally from the diet. The various stages of food energy utilization from storage to starvation are shown in Figure 4. In the transition from the fed to the fasted state the sequence of metabolic events that occur and their approximate durations are outlined in Table 8. The subdivisions shown overlap the examples a–d described in Figure 4. It should be noted that throughout this section the implication is that fat reserves are substantial since this was the case in the original experimental studies.

TABLE 8

PHASES OF STARVATION

|  | Duration |
|---|---|
| 1) Gastro-Intestinal Absorption | 1-6 hours |
| 2) Glycogenolysis | ca. 1 day |
| 3) Gluconeogenesis | 1 week |
| 4) Ketosis | from day 3 |
| 5) Gluconeogenesis Decreased Brain Ketone Utilization Significant | from 2nd week |

Source: Cahil (1978)

When a normal meal containing carbohydrate is consumed, storage takes place and the routes of utilization of the elevated circulating glucose are shown in Figure 4a. Insulin levels rise and the entire body oxidizes glucose for a period. The elevation of insulin accompanied by reduced glucagon also allows rapid uptake of glucose by the liver. These routes involving both storage and utilization are:

$$Glucose \longrightarrow G6P \longrightarrow Pyruvate \longrightarrow Acetyl\ CoA \longrightarrow CO_2 \quad + Energy$$
$$\uparrow \qquad \qquad \updownarrow$$
$$\longrightarrow Glycogen \qquad FA \longleftrightarrow TG$$

Glycogen stores remain in the liver but triglycerides (TG) are normally exported to adipose tissue through the blood mainly as very low density lipoproteins (VLDL).

Muscle generally uses fatty acids (FA) as its preferred source of energy but immediately following a meal when blood glucose levels are high and FA low, the latter due to insulin effects on adipose tissue via cyclic adenosine monophosphate (cAMP), glucose is used both for replenishing depleted glycogen reserves as well as being oxidized for energy.

In adipose tissue insulin stimulates glucose uptake and its conversion into FA via Acetyl CoA. At the same time high levels of insulin (and hence low glucagon and low cAMP) inhibit lipolysis and favor triglyceride (TG) storage. Because the adipose cell has no glycerokinase, glycerol cannot be used for resynthesis of TG. When glucose is high, cAMP is low and TG synthesis is favored. Brain glucose utilization continues, as was the case before feeding, by direct uptake from blood glucose.

At the same time, although not shown in the diagram, amino acids from dietary protein will join the blood amino acid pool via the portal supply and would allow, again under insulin control, tissue amino acid uptake and replenishment of peripheral protein. Simultaneously, amino acids, when in excess to immediate protein synthetic needs, are deaminated and their carbon skeletons join the carbohydrate metabolic routes at various points depending on the structure of the original amino acid concerned (Fig 3). Fat is transported mainly as chylomicra via the lymphatics and under influence of various lipoprotein lipases joins newly synthesized fatty acids as part of the stored TG in adipose tissue. Meals of abnormal composition, especially when very low in carbohydrate, may initiate different responses.

Several hours after a meal the elevated levels of glucose, amino acids and chylomicra would have declined to normal levels and utilization of stored glucose and fat begins. Total free body glucose amounts to only 15 grams (60 Kcal) which is only about one hour of utilization at a basal need of 1 Kcal/min. (Cahill 1978). Sensitive mechanisms thus exist to allow glucose utilization to proceed as required but also to allow circulating levels to remain approximately constant. Again insulin/glucagon ratios and cellular levels of cAMP are the major control mechanisms involved. From Figure 4b it will be seen that liver begins to return its stored glucose (glycogen) as free glucose to the bloodstream. This is dependent on glucose-6-phosphatase being present in the liver. The breakdown of glycogen to glucose and its release is controlled by two linked factors: reduced portal glucose and reduced insulin.

During this phase of decreasing glucose and insulin levels, peripheral tissues such as muscle and adipose tissue progressively reduce glucose utilization so that after 8-10 hours over 50% of muscle fuel are met by free fatty acid (FFA) oxidation (Cahill 1978). At the same time in adipose tissue (Figure 4b) since insulin levels are reduced, cAMP increases causing TG breakdown and thus increased fatty acid release. The glycerol produced cannot be reutilized for TG synthesis in adipose tissue due to lack of the appropriate kinase to manufacture glycerol-3-phosphate (G3P) from glycerol and must be exported to the liver for utilization either in glucose production or in TG synthesis. Muscle glycogen can supply muscle energy needs and can be partially recycled as lactic acid but since glucose-6-phosphatase is lacking in muscle, glucose release from muscle glycogen does not occur.

The next stage of adaptation is shown in Figure 4c which represents the condition following an overnight fast. The utilization of glycogen and fat continues but two additional phenomena become more important both of which continue as starvation proceeds; these are gluconeogensis and ketogenesis.

**Gluconeogenesis:**

Gluconeogensis is described as the formation of glucose from non-carbohydrate precursors and is outlined in Figure 5. When dietary intakes of fat, carbohydrate and protein are below requirements then adaptations occur to spare the most critical components of the body and to use the most expendable. The most expendable material for energy use is stored fat and this is used throughout deprivation. Muscle protein (the largest protein reserve) is also an energy reserve but there are long term constraints on its use. Lack of dietary protein with adequate dietary energy produces different adaptations and these will be discussed elsewhere. Glucose is normally the major or sole energy source for the brain and nervous system, red and white blood cells, active fibroblasts and certain phagocytes (Levenson and Seifter 1973). Glucose synthesis in the body during starvation is, therefore, essential since glucose and glucogen stores are extremely small. Cahill (1978) has calculated that liver glycogen can maintain blood glucose for 12–16 hours and in the post–absorptive state, (Figure 4c), glycogen may supply about 75% of the splanchnic glucose output with gluconeogensis providing the remainder. The brain normally oxidizes glucose completely to carbon dioxide and water via acetyl coenzyme A and the tricarboxylic acid cycle. In other tissues without mitochondria, glycolysis through to lactate may predominate with the liver and kidney converting the lactate back to glucose.

The changes that allow increased glycogen utilization are triggered by falling levels of blood glucose which begins to decrease from average levels of 75 mg/100 ml at about 15 hours after feeding. Insulin levels also begin to fall about this time, while in contrast glucagon levels are rising. The increased glucagon/insulin ratio stimulates both glycogen breakdown in the liver and FA release from adipose tissue both mediated by elevated cAMP levels. These liver and adipose tissue changes are accompanied by increased use of muscle proteins a source of amino acids for glucose production. After about three days of starvation, 24 hour substrate turnover estimates show significant amounts of glucose from splanchnic glucose production, part of which would have originated from muscle proteolysis. The use of various substrates as energy sources is also illustrated in Figure 6. Most of the energy used originates from TG with protein supplying most of the glucose. The important diversion through ketone bodies (KB) production will be discussed below. The limited contribution of glycerol as a source of glucose should be noted. In experimental animals at least, some small amount of glucose may also originate from fatty acids via acetoacetate and acetone by an incompletely defined route (see Cahill 1981).

Muscle is a significant energy store and has an important metabolic role throughout starvation. This role has been reviewed by Levenson and

Seifter (1984) who cite several adaptive mechanisms involving muscle protein. These include:

a) **Muscle Creatine Phosphate:** In starvation, muscle contraction activity is reduced to near basal levels. A creatine phosphate reservoir, while an extremely useful mechanism in nourished active muscle, may well be inappropriate in the starving cell. Reduction in the activity of the creatine kinase system may be associated with muscle wasting and thus not only may there be a reduction in the amount of work that muscle can perform (an important adaptive response to increase survival time) but there may be also inhibition of the adenosine triphosphate (ATP) dependent phases of glucose assimilation so as to conserve glucose for brain and blood cell metabolism.

b) **Muscle Glycogensis:** Even in the absence of glucose there is a limited capacity to synthesize glycogen from those amino acids that can be readily converted to oxaloacetate (OAA). This ability, however, has the liability of high energy cost. The conversion takes place at different stages in both cytosol and mitochondria and involves mitochondrial phosphoenolpyruvate carboxykinase together with guanosine triphosphate (GTP) to produce phosphoenolpyruvate (PEP) from OAA. The high energy cost precludes its extensive use in starvation and in addition specific mechanisms limit amino acid availability for this purpose.

c) **Amino Acid Cycles:** Alanine has a key role in coupling amino acid metabolism with glucose metabolism. This cycle (Figure 7) analogous to the Cori (lactate) cycle was first described by Felig and his associates (1970, 1973). Another important cycle is the glutamate-glutamine cycle (Marliss et al 1971) also shown in Figure 7. These cycles both provide additional alanine to the liver for glucose production. The control of blood amino acid levels in man has been reviewed by Cahill et al (1981), who indicate the complexity of the relationships by suggesting that 'everything more or less' regulates amino acid concentrations in the circulation.

In the glucose–alanine cycle the muscle alanine is produced both from transamination of pyruvate and by proteolysis. The amino acids for transamination are mainly the branched–chain amino acids with the keto–acids being metabolized for energy:

Following exercise or fasting there is increased muscle pyruvate production, alanine release to the liver, and hence increased substrate availability for gluconeogenesis. The glucose–alanine cycle, however, does not account for a new flow of amino acid carbon to carbohydrate during starvation. Levensen and Seifter (1983) indicate that the increased carbon efflux from muscle is derived principally from the metabolic transformation of amino acids to alanine and glutamine. While such transformations can involve the majority of protein amino acids the branched chain amino acids have a special role since muscle can utilize leucine, isoleucine and valine to a greater extent than the liver. In addition, some of the keto compounds produced following transamination may act as regulators by inhibiting muscle breakdown.

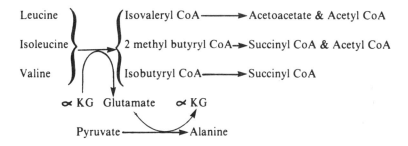

The role of glutamine and the glutamine–glutamate cycle (Figure 7) is critical since kidney is also a major site for gluconeogenesis. While in short term starvation most gluconeogenesis takes place in the liver, at later stages the liver and kidney become of almost equal importance with glutamine being the prime substrate for this renal gluconeogenesis. The kidney thus has the ability to dispose of both the carbon and the nitrogen arriving as glutamine from the muscle—the former to glucose, the latter to ammonia. Urea synthesis in the liver requires energy; excretion of ammonia from the kidney uses less energy and also contributes to the homeostasis of acid base balance. Ammonium can thus become the major nitrogen excretory product in advanced starvation (Cahill 1970); this however, is dependent on the degree of depletion experienced and the original fat stores present. In normal urine (Keys *et al* 1950) about 90% of the nitrogen is excreted as urea with the proportion decreasing to about 70% during the first week of starvation where it may then remain for two weeks or more. In other early studies (Knack and Neuman, 1917, and Kohn 1920), ammonia nitrogen represented only 7–9% of the nitrogen. The latter study was on one subject who received only 825 Kcal/day. There are undoubtedly considerable differences in the partition of nitrogen observed between zero intake where body tissue must supply all daily needs and semi-starvation where tissue use is less. The total daily nitrogen (N) excretion of this subject was 5.25 gN/day while in one of Succi's prolonged fasts (see Keys *et al* 1950) nitrogen excretion at the 20th day of starvation had dropped to about 3 gN/day. The excretion of nitrogen on N free diets, but with adequate calories, shows that the professional faster (Succi) was using only little more N than subjects on a non–protein diet.

Ketogenesis and gluconeogenesis are overlapping phases in the early stages of starvation with the latter declining as starvation progresses. This is because the large losses of nitrogen observed in the early stages of starvation of 12 g or more per day (Cahill 1978) are unsustainable and thus a second phase must supervene which allows greater fat utilization in pathways where formally glucose use predominated. This allows reduced gluconeogenesis from muscle and thus protein conservation. The pool of free fatty acids enlarges with both muscle and liver increasing their utilization. The fatty acids are fully oxidized in muscle and up to 90% of calorie use may be from this source (Levenson and Seifter 1983). In liver, in contrast, energy is produced by beta-oxidation to acetyl CoA with this then being exported in the form of the ketone bodies (KB): acetoacetate and beta-hydroxybutyrate. These two compounds are sometimes termed the 3-oxybutyrates (KB). The reactions involved and their regulation, outlined in Figures 8 and 9, are dependent on the balance between glucose and free fatty acid availability. Partial oxidation in the liver to KB is an effective means of disposal of FA while at the same time providing energy in the form of 3-oxybutyrates for extrahepatic tissues. This allows sparing of glucose as a metabolic fuel in muscle, allowing it to be used in the brain and red blood cells (RBC). Acetone (formed from acetoacetate) may be lost in the lungs and the 3-oxybutyrates (with the hydroxy compound predominating) may be lost in the urine. As KB production increases so also does the proportion of nitrogen excreted as $[NH_4]'$ thus contributing to acid-base balance. The steps involved in the production of the KB from acetyl CoA are:

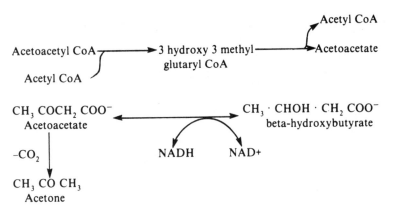

The concentrations of acetoacetate and beta-hydroxybutyrate in a resting individual are sensitive indicators of the dependence on fatty acids as fuel. During fasting there is a marked rise in the concentration of these compounds in the blood and urine. Ketoacid production by the splanchnic bed is maximal by the third day of starvation (Garber et al 1974) but blood levels increase until about two weeks (Cahill et al 1966). This is probably mainly due to decreased muscle utilization of KB (Owen and Reichard 1971). The control for these increases in KB production by the liver (Cahill 1978) is the result of a higher glucagon/insulin ratio together with an increase of free fatty acids released from adipose tissue.

In more advanced starvation, as is outlined in Figure 4d, the major adaptive change is that the brain is able to use KB for fuel. Associated with this, gluconeogenesis from muscle has declined together with reduced KB use by muscle.

It is not known for certain whether the intellectual and/or emotional changes noted in starvation are directly caused by the use of a much greater proportion of keto acids for fuel. In the Minnesota experiment, intellectual function was little changed (although depression increased) as semi-starvation proceeded. However, despite an average 25% weight loss produced by the 24 weeks of restriction there was no excessive production of KB at any state of the experiment. No tests were performed to ascertain whether increased brain use of KB had taken place, thus the psychological and intellectual changes observed cannot be used to answer the question posed above. Two effects are described by Cahill (1978) when KB are used extensively by the brain for fuel: the elevation of the electroconvulsive threshold and some unspecified but significant changes in the hypothalamic area of the brain.

Although protein losses may have been as high as 75 g daily early in starvation (the stores in Table 7 would last only 40 days at this rate of breakdown), these losses will have been reduced to less than 20 g daily in prolonged starvation. This reduction prevents protein depletion becoming critical before fat stores are exhausted. The data from Grande 1968 (Table 9) show that the caloric value of tissue lost late in starvation is greater than the tissue lost earlier. This is a reflection of the increasing utilization of body fat as starvation proceeds. Initially a mixture of fat, protein and

TABLE 9

CALORIC EQUIVALENT OF WEIGHT LOSS

| Days of Negative Energy Balance | Caloric Equivalent Kcal/Kg | Approximate Composition |
|---|---|---|
| 1-3 | 2596 | Water-Protein-Fat |
| 11-13 | 7043 | Mainly Fat |
| 22-24 | 87900 | Mainly Fat |

Caloric Equivalent of the weight loss (Kcal/Kg) is calculated by dividing the caloric deficit by the weight loss. The caloric deficit is computed as the difference between the total caloric expenditures and the metabolizable energy of the diet. Intake ca. 1000 Kcal/day, Expenditure ca. 3200 Kcal/day.
Source: Grande (1968).

water is used, while in the later stages the loss is similar to the theoretical value for adipose tissue.

The enzyme changes illustrated in Table 10 are derived from rat studies, but are likely to be similar in humans. Most of the changes fit with expectations. Starvation diminishes the need for digestion, for conversion of glucose to fatty acids and for storage of fatty acids in adipose tissue. At the same time there is increased fatty acid utilization and, at least in the early stages, an increase in gluconeogenesis from amino acids. Fatty acid utilization in the mitochondria of muscle cells requires enzymes to allow the transfer across the mitochondrial membranes. These are two forms of carnitine acyl transferase and the fatty acyl CoA so transferred can then follow the beta-oxidation route to acetyl CoA. The mechanism involves carnitine $[(CH_3)_3N'\ CH_2\text{-}CHOH\text{-}CH_2\text{-}COO^-]$ a N-containing compound which requires methyl groups from methionine and a carbon chain from lysine—two essential amino acids—for its synthesis (Broquist et al 1975). It is of interest that carnitine levels in muscle have been shown to increase in starving dogs and humans (Levenson and Seifter 1983).

The switch from glucose utilization to fatty acid utilization is controlled in part by KB which inhibit the activity of pyruvate dehydrogenase as also do increased levels of acetyl CoA. Levenson and Seifter (1983) conclude that "whereas in the first phase (of starvation) the drop in insulin secretion and increase in glucagon are at the basis of the metabolic adaptations that occur, in the second phase the ketone bodies play a dual role: on the one hand they represent a major energy substrate; on the other hand they also play a major regulatory role in this metabolic adaptation particularly in depressing gluconeogenesis". The regulatory importance of KB in natural starvation where fat stores are not excessive is less clearly established.

Acute infection, on even previously well nourished subjects (Cerra et al 1983), superimposes major hormonal changes on those of starvation (reduced intake also caused by the sepsis) and produces dramatically changed metabolic-physiologic responses which may threaten survival. The interactions of nutrition and infection in Third World situations where previous nutritional status may have been marginal or worse is thus of fundamental importance.

## Starvation, Malnutrition and Resistance to Infection

The documentation of a synergistic relationship between malnutrition and infection (Scrimshaw et al 1968) fundamentally changed the way in which potential solutions to the problems of world malnutrition were viewed. No longer could food and nutrients be considered in isolation but

# TABLE 10

## ENZYME ADAPTATIONS TO STARVATION

| INCREASED Name | Role | DECREASED Name | Role |
|---|---|---|---|
| *Pancreatic Enzymes* | | | |
| None | | All hydrolytic | |
| *Fatty Acid Synthetic Enzymes* | | | |
| None | | Acetyl CoA carboxylase | Acetyl CoA to Malonyl CoA |
| | | Fatty Acid synthase | Chain lengthening |
| | | Acyl CoA desaturate (L) | Double bond insertion |
| | | Lipoprotein lipase (A) | TG uptake |
| | | NADP-Malatedehydrogenase | NADPH for FA synthesis |
| | | Citrate lyase | Citrate to Acetyl CoA and OAA |
| *Fatty Acid Utilization* | | | |
| Carnitine Acyl Transferase (L) | FA transfer | None | |
| 3 Keto Acid CoA transferase (B) | KB utilization | | |
| NAD coupled dehydrogenase (B) | KB utilization | | |
| *Glucose Utilization* | | | |
| None | | Glucokinase (L) | Liver Glucose uptake |
| *Gluconeogenesis form Amino Acid* | | | |
| Serine dehydratase | Serine to Pyruvate | None | |
| Alanine Amino transferase | Alanine to Pyruvate | | |
| Pyruvate carboxylase | Pyruvate to OAA | | |
| PEP carboxykinase | OAA to PEP | | |
| Glucose 6 phosphatase | G6P to Glucose | | |

A = Adipose Tissue   B = Brain   L = Liver
The enzymes listed are selective and include only the more significant changes.
Adapted from McGilvery (1982).

they became interwined with social and sanitation factors and hence with the fundamentals of the development process (Latham 1975, Pellett 1983).

How infection influences the pathogenesis of protein–energy malnutrition (P–EM)is misleadingly precise; kwashiorkor and marasmus arise as the result of a whole range of dietary and environmental insults, infection playing a major role. Infections not only accelerate the pathogenesis of protein–energy malnutrition by increasing the rate of weight loss or by introducing protein–losing enteropathy, they can also reverse the course of the pathogenesis so that kwashiorkor appears in circumstances in which marasmus would be expected, and vice–versa. Infection interacts with diet at a number of stages; it may affect appetite, cause nutrient loss via diarrhoea and vomiting, result in plasma protein loss via the gut and influence the metabolic fate of absorbed nutrients by altering hormonal balance. Diet may also affect the course of infectious disease by impairing the immune response."

Chen (1983) describes the mutual interaction of diarrhoea and malnutrition in a similar manner: "Diarrhoea causes, precipitates or exacerbates energy–protein malnutrition and conversely, malnutrition predisposes and worsens diarrhoea". The strategies with which UNICEF (UNICEF 1984) is now fighting malnutrition in Third World countries for which the mnemonic GOBI is sometimes used: Growth monitoring, Oral rehydration therapy, Breast feeding encouragement and Immunization programs, are an implicit recognition of these interrelationships. In a similar manner to Whitehead (1981), Chandra (1982) and Chen (1983) describe four mechanisms whereby an infective agent such as E. coli, Shigella or Rotavirus can affect the nutritional status of a child. These would be via food intake (reduced), nutrient absorption (reduced), metabolic loss (catabolism increased) and direct losses (eg protein and micronutrient losses increased). The reverse effect, that is the influence of nutritional status on the ability to withstand infection, is also important but is less clearcut. The most commonly identified effect is of malnutrition on immunocompetence (Scrimshaw 1975, Douglas 1981, Chandra 1981, Chandra 1982, Chen and Scrimshaw 1982, Chen 1983). In field studies, protein–energy malnutrition is accompanied by profound immuno–deficiency (Gross and Newburne 1980) involving both T cell–mediated immunity and humoral immunity. Experimental studies do not always reproduce these findings and it has been suggested that the T cell-mediated immuno–deficiency seen in field studies may be attributable to concomitant deficiencies of zinc (Golden *et al* 1978, Hansen *et al* 1982).

Diarrhoea of various etiologies is highly associated with the pathogenesis of protein–energy malnutrition (Chen 1978, 1983) and there is good evidence that disease severity is greater in the malnourished (Chen and Scrimshaw 1982). Resistance to infection in both human and animal studies as a consequence of starvation is discussed by Levenson and Seifter (1983) who cite examples pertaining to levels of circulating antibodies, to atrophy of lymphoid tissue and depression of cellular immunity, to reduction of the inflammatory responses and to histological effects on the bone marrow. In addition to the effects of malnutrition on infection, P–EM may increase the host's susceptibility to parasitic infestation by various routes which include specific immune defense (antibodies and lymphoid system) as well as non–specific factors such as epithelial and mucous membrane permeability, complement components and the role of metallic chelators. Many examples of these interactions are given by Isliker and Schurch (1981).

The understanding of these interrelationships now gives the potential for intervention to save the lives of children to a degree not previously possible. Diarrhoea at present accounts for 20–35% of childhood deaths in developing countries together with a substantial portion of the growth retardation of the surviving children. However, control of the diarrhoea-malnutrition complex must integrate an undertanding of both social organization and health technology (Chen 1983). Interventions such that the infant mortality rate due to diarrhoea and malnutrition could be substantially reduced are well within our present technology, (UNICEF 1984, Feachem and Koblinsky 1984) but whether such undertakings are within our moral, social and political capabilities remains unfortunately another issue.

**Protein-Energy Malnutrition**

Protein-Energy Malnutrition (P-EM) has been defined by WHO (1973) as a range of pathological conditions arising from coincidental lack, in varying proportions, of protein and calories, occurring most frequently in infants and young children and commonly associated with infections. The conditions concerned can be said to range in severity from mild through moderate to severe. Certainly the mild, and probably also the moderate, degrees are subclinical and can only be detected by anthro pometric (Waterlow et al 1977) biochemical and perhaps functional tests (Calloway 1977, Solomons and Allan 1983). The early stages are characterized by growth failure and possibly some retardation of mental development (Brozek 1982). The severity of degree of P-EM ranges in type of clinical picture in a graded fashion (Jelliffe 1959, McLaren et al 1967). Two distinct syndromes occur at either end of the spectrum, Marasmus and Kwashiorkor; in between varying degrees of each are found in what is termed Marasmic-Kwashiorkor. Severe marasmus, usually precipitated by a severe infectious episode, is characterized by growth retardation, very low plasma insulin levels, loss of body fat, and muscle wasting. When total caloric intake has been adequate or nearly adequate, as is possible when starchy low-protein foods are dietary staples, the symptoms include pellagra-type dermatitis, fatty liver, changes in texture and pigmentation of hair, gastro-intestinal disturbances, and diarrhoea with resulting loss of electrolytes. Infections are involved in the precipitation of both conditions but it is believed by Whitehead (1981) that the severity and type of the associated infection can induce change from the Marasmic end of the spectrum to the Kwashiorkor end.

Conclusions on the prevalence of severe P-EM are generally drawn from both anthropometric data, where a criterion of less than 60% of a given reference weight for age has been used and from clinical criteria. In both sets of studies the prevalence of P-EM ranged from about 4% of children examined in community surveys to about 30% in severely poverty-stricken areas (Bengoa 1973). The total numbers of children suffering from P-EM can be estimated from recent population studies and the earlier regional prevalence data from Bengoa and Donoso (1974). Estimates are of course dependent on the definition used, but the total of 87 million would rise to 200 million or more if stunted growth were included in the definition. For infants and young children, the risk of dying is very closely related to the conditions of the environment in which they live; infants in low-income groups thus experience higher infant mortality rates than those in other income groups. Other factors of importance in the pathogenesis of P-EM are family socio-economic status and place of residence, methods of infant feeding, environmental sanitation, housing conditions, and cultural beliefs and customs. Harfouche (1979) estimates that 60% to 80% of all infant deaths occur in the post-neonatal period, the time when deaths are caused mainly by an interaction between infections and malnutrition.

As has been discussed earlier, adaptation to food deficiency allows maintenance of homeostasis for prolonged periods. Evolution has allowed this adaptation to become an extremely efficient protective procedure. The breakdown of muscle permits transamination to occur with amino acids, especially alanine, thus available to the liver for gluconeogenesis. Muscle breakdown also supplies amino acids to the liver allowing almost normal synthesis of the serum protein to albumin. Normal levels of serum albumin allow osmotic balance; thus edema does not occur and consequently in Marasmus the metabolic abnormalities other than wasting are few. (Figure 10.)

In contrast, human adaptation to low protein–high carbohydrate diets appears much less beneficial and metabolic derangements become quickly apparent (Alleyn *et al* 1977). One might hazard an opinion that agriculture and thus the possibility of consuming low protein–high calorie diets would be so recent in human evolution that efficient adaptations have not arisen. A distorted serum amino acid pool in Kwashiorkor (but not in Marasmus) has been long recognized (Whitehead and Alleyne,

1972). This may be caused by insulin induced movement of amino acids into the muscle accompanied by continued activity of the protein synthetic pathways. The distorted serum amino acid pool thus produced, results in a distorted liver amino pool and hence poor albumin synthesis (Whitehead and Alleyne 1972, Coward and Lunn 1981). Hypoalbuminemia, while not the sole causative factor, is often related to increased levels of extra-cellular fluid and frank edema. In addition, the distorted liver amino acid pool does not permit adequate synthesis of the very low density lipoproteins (VLDL) and low density lipoproteins (LDL) fractions necessary for the transport of triglycerides and other lipids from the liver (Fig 10, right). This, when accompanied by high carbohydrate consumption and hence high lipid production in the liver, precipitates the fatty infiltration of Kwashiorkor where in extreme cases 50% of the weight of the liver may be fat.

This outline is extremely oversimplified and does not include consideration of other changes in carbohydrate and lipid metabolism (Alleyne *et al* 1972, 1977, Truswell 1975), the complex additional relationships between hormone balance (Coward and Lunn 1981) malnutrition and infection (Whitehead 1981) and the simultaneous deficiency of minerals and/or vitamins (Solomons 1985). Other differences and similarities between marasmus and kwashiorkor are shown in Table 11. The biochemical and clinical manifestations of P-EM have been reviewed by Jelliffe (1959), McLaren and Pellett (1970), Waterlow and Alleyne (1977), Coward and Lunn (1981), Torun Viteri 1984 and Waterlow (1984).

Aflatoxins in foods and their effects on the liver have been also suggested as additional factors in the pathogenesis of kwashiorkor (Hendrickse *et al* 1982). While the evidence for association in some circumstances appears conclusive there is general agreement that this is not the major causative route (Anon. 1984a,b) and that the classical explanations (Whitehead and Alleyne 1972, Coward and Lunn 1981), while certainly not all-embracing, must be accepted for the present. There are a large number of variable factors (similar to those discussed below in relation to food deprivation) affecting all three areas of agent, host and environment; thus it is not surprising that a large number of anomalies exist not only in the biochemical and clinical symptoms observed, but also in the role of diet in the causation of P-EM.

Although severe protein energy malnutrition is diagnosed on both anthropometric and on clinical criteria, the mild and moderate forms can only be identified by use of anthropometric standards. While weight for age deficits have been of immense value, in classifying malnutrition, the procedure is limited in that it is unable to distinguish between the acute and chronic malnutrition and can thus overestimate the prevalence of the problem. This was indicated in Table 4 where the proportions defined as malnourished differ widely when different criteria are used for classification. Recent expert committees on growth monitoring and nutritional surveillance have recommended the use of height for age and weight for height as additional indicators of nutritional status in children (Waterlow *et al* 1977, Mason *et al* 1984).

TABLE 11

SOME COMPARISONS BETWEEN MARASMUS AND KWASHIORKOR

| Feature | Marasmus | Kwashiorkor |
|---|---|---|
| **GENERAL** | | |
| Incidence | Worldwide | Regional |
| Age | Less than 1 year | 1-2 years |
| **CLINICAL SIGNS** | | |
| Edema | Absent | Present |
| Dermatosis | Rare | Common |
| Enlarged liver | Common | Very Common |
| Muscle and fat wasting | Severe | Mild |
| Stunting | Severe | Moderate |
| Anemia | Common and severe | Mild |
| **BIOCHEMICAL SIGNS** | | |
| Total body water | High | High |
| Extracellular water | Moderate | High |
| Body potassium | Some depletion | Much depletion |
| Fatty liver | Absent | Common and severe |
| Serum proteins | Slightly low | Very low |
| Serum albumin | Slightly low | Very low |
| Essential amino acids/ Nonessential amino acids | Normal | Reduced |
| LDL | Normal | Low |
| Nonesterified fatty acids | Normal | High |

Source: Adapted from D.S. McLaren and P.L. Pellet (1970).

Until relatively recently, although the less prevalent condition, Kwashiorkor had received more attention than Marasmus partly because of the large variety of biochemical abnormalities associated with it. Greater emphasis is now being placed on the socio–economic and political aspects of malnutrition (Pellett 1983), to the clarification of the energy and protein relationships in health and disease (Viteri *et al* 1979, Torun *et al* 1981, Rand *et al* 1984) and to simple methods of prevention and treatment such as those described under the GOBI mnemonic (UNICEF 1984) referred to earlier in relation to nutrition and infection.

# EPILOGUE

Starvation causes major changes in the external actions and attributes of the body as well as in its internal functioning. All of these changes can be considered as favoring survival in the face of a challenge to life. Activity, basal metabolic rate and body size are reduced and the use of energy reserves is modified, so as to use the reserves most efficiently. These changes are all adaptations to promote survival but as yet in this review no attempt has been made to define the concept of adaptation.

Following in the steps of Cannon (1932) adaptation has been defined by Waterlow (1975) as an 'adjustment of the organism that enables it to maintain normal structure and function under different environmental conditions'. Three refinements are recognized. These are a) adaptation is relatively slow in contrast to the rapid, repeated regulatory processes which control homeostasis, b) the normal can itself include a component of adaptation but still remain normal, and c) some parameters vary a great deal more than others within the range of normalcy and thus judicious selection of the parameters to measure, together with care in drawing conclusions is necessary.

The adaptations that have been outlined earlier are derived both from experimentation and from observation and appear true for the conditions described. Nonetheless, adaptations to starvation can vary enormously and qualifications have been made throughout earlier sections. Observed changes are in practice dependent, both in degree and in kind, on a large number of variables, many of which are interdependent. These include:

1. The degree of dietary energy restriction in relation to previous habitual intake: ie how severe, how variable and for how long was the restriction experienced?

2. The nutritional quality of the food actually consumed; its composition especially in relation to protein, minerals and vitamins and the degree of variability of food quality experienced over the deprivation period.

3. The level and frequency of activity undertaken and the environmental conditions, especially temperature and humidity.

4. The water supply both in its quality and its quantity.

5. The previous nutritional state and the levels of stores present in the body. This variable is particularly important since many of the bio-

chemical studies have been performed on subjects with high fat stores.

6. The age and physiological status of the individual experiencing deprivation: growth, pregnancy and/or lactation requirements will be additional to normal needs and will thus not only affect the degree of deprivation but also the factors affected by the deprivation.

7. The state of health of the individual; are injury, trauma, infestation and especially infection present? The type, length and severity of the infection and/or trauma will affect hormonal status and hence the adaptations experienced.

8. Any additional physiological or psychological stresses received during deprivation which may also influence hormonal status.

It is thus not surprising that while there are many phenomena common to nutritional deprivation in general there are also many biochemical and physiological responses that vary significantly. It will usually be true that when major contradictions exist in the literature of malnutrition and starvation, the reason will be found in the host, diet and environmental variables cited above.

Famine involves many additional factors including emotional as well as psychological trauma and may thus differ considerably from the experimental. This was well recognized by Keys *et al* (1950) in their study of experimental starvation. Nonetheless conclusions reached under 'clean' experimental conditions are important in interpreting the finding found in famine when degradation, deprivation and disease are rife. Such information can also be basic to famine relief operations to ease suffering and speed recovery. Unfortunately this knowledge can do little to prevent such tragedies from occurring.

When one has seen the gross sufferings caused by famine, hunger and malnutrition it is easy to feel that biochemical and physiological research has little relevance since the root causes are in the lack of economic and social development and that real solutions lie only in the political sphere. Nevertheless increases in our understanding of nutritional needs, of the adaptations experienced in malnutrition and of the interactions between nutrition and infection do allow activities to proceed which can improve health, reduce mortality and improve nutritional status within the economic constraints imposed. The justice or otherwise of the constraints is considered by some as irrelevant since these constraints to action exist and are likely to change only slowly, if at all. Others would say that acceptance of the constraints perpetuates the system and should be resisted.

Ethical and moral dilemmas abound for those in food, nutrition and developmental activity (Stumpf 1981, Schuftan 1983) and there are many ways of reacting to them (George 1975, Lappe and Collins 1977, McLaren 1983). In Table 12, adapted in part from Pinstrup-Andersen (1983), some of the steps in the sequence of events which define an individual's nutritional status are shown together with some of the major factors that affect them. Little can be done by nutritionists to increase food or money availability at the family level. These actions rest in the domains of politics, economics and agricultural production. By increased knowledge of food more nutrients can however be obtained for the same food expenditure. Deficiencies of food allocation within the family can also be recognized; the vulnerable groups are women, both during pregnancy and lactation, and the young growing child. Finally, food utilization depends upon a healthy and sanitary environment. Thus, on a limited and local scale, individual nutritional status can be improved despite our being unable to

TABLE 12

SCHEMATIC OVERVIEW OF SOME MAJOR FACTORS
AFFECTING NUTRITIONAL STATUS

| Sequence | Some Causes and/or Solutions |
| --- | --- |
| Food availability | International and national politics and economics, agricultural policy, production and distribution. |
| ↓ | |
| Family purchasing power | Political and economic factors at a local level: Targeted economic assistance will help improve purchasing power. |
| ↓ | |
| Family food purchasing pattern | Poor nutrition knowledge: Nutrition education will result in improved food selection. |
| ↓ | |
| Within family food distribution | Poor nutrition knowledge: Nutrition education and targeted food assistance will result in improved food distribution. |
| ↓ | |
| Utilization of foods by consumer | Infection, infestation, poor sanitation: Health advice and services will result in improved food utilization |
| ↓ | |
| Individual nutritional status | |

Source: P.L. Pellet (1983).

affect, in marked degree, the basic societal causes of poverty and malnutrition (Pellett 1983). Nevertheless, while one can and must act at the micro level, it should be recognized not only that the priority given to agriculture is far too low in many developing countries but also that 'generating employment and income for the poor is essential to the solution of hunger and malnutrition. It is not enough to grow more food crops if the poor and hungry consumer has not ability to purchase it. The deeply-rooted poverty in the low-income, densely populated countries remains the greatest single impediment to the eradiction of hunger' (UNU, 1982).

Population growth itself is in the long term an even greater threat since this directly affects all other activities. Thus food and nutrition become part of the overall development issue and are dependent on governmental actions for their improvement; they are, therefore, part of the political spectrum and it would be naive to assume otherwise. Unfortunately, moral dimensions have a habit of becoming lost when national and political considerations arise.

These dilemmas are recognized widely, yet our inaction on all but the most limited scale continues. Many of the same arguments concerning the respective roles of government and private enterprise currently propounded, surfaced during the Irish Famine of the 1840's (Woodham-Smith 1962). Even further in the past, Dando (1983) cites a similar sequence of causes for many of the Biblical famines as those occurring today. The victims also remain the same—'to those that have not, more shall be taken away', apparently reflecting our view of international justice.

It seems at times impossible to believe that our scientific abilities and our moral attributes concerning food, nutrition, health and development can exist on the same planet at the same time. Yet for the future, cooperation is essential between rich and poor, North and South and East and West, but real cooperation seems as far away as ever. It is difficult to be other than a pessimist when one sees the present state of the world and the resounding disinterest shown by many of the richer nations to the very reasonable and modest suggestions put forward by the Brandt Commission (1980). Behind everything loom the traditional questions of peace and war and the massive expenditures on armaments which take resources away from urgent needs. To quote from the Commission Report:

"There is a real danger that in the year 2000 a large part of the world's population will still be living in poverty. This world may become overpopulated and will certainly be overurbanized. Mass starvation and the dangers of destruction may be growing steadily. The aims of the future must be to diminish the distance between rich and poor nations, to do away with discrimination, to approach equality of opportunities step by step. This is not only a matter of striving for justice, which in itself would be important, but it is also sound self-interest not only for the poor and very poor nations, but for the better off as well".

Thus in conclusion, our scientific knowledge on the physiology and biochemistry of hunger and malnutrition, while far from complete, is sufficient to understand the majority of the major effects produced. We also comprehend the basic reasons that allow hunger and starvation to occur. Our capacity, however, for acting upon and eliminating these causes remains as shortsighted and sometimes even antagonistic to such actions as ever. As Brozek (1982) remarks 'The war on hunger is such a difficult task because it is inseparable from the war on poverty'. The reason for inaction is that the political will in the community is not present. Those of us in science, medicine and agriculture are generally unprepared and badly equipped to enter and fight for actions in the political sphere. These paradoxes and realities are recognised by Mayer (1985). 'In this century the world has acquired the scientific basis and the technology to predict, mitigate, and eventually prevent famines. I am convinced, however, that little will happen without a concerted and continuing political effort on the part of the scientific and technological community'.

I believe Jean Mayer to be correct in this assessment; political efforts must be intensified by the scientific community who recognise the achievements and possibilities but who are also aware of how few of these achievements are really helping those in desperate need. Action is needed now and time is not on our side.

Peter L. Pellett, professor of food science and nutrition at the University of Massachusetts, is widely recognized as an expert on malnutrition and starvation. Educated in England, he received the Ph.D. in nutrition from the London School of Hygiene and Tropical Medicine. He has been on the faculty of the American University of Beirut and has served as a consultant on problems of nutrition and agricultural development in Libya, Syria, Lebanon, Lagos, Kuwait, Nigeria, Sudan, Iraq, and Jordan. He has written extensively on the causes and effects of starvation.

# FIGURES

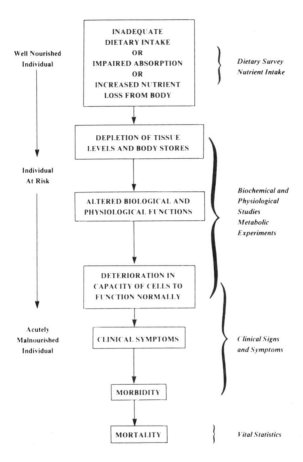

Figure 1: **Major Stages in the Development of Nutritional Deficiency Disease.**
Nutritional deficiency begins with an inadequate availability of a nutrient to body cells and organs. This inadequacy may be due to various factors, including low dietary intakes or relatively high rates of loss from the body. Subsequently biochemical deterioration occurs with the appearance of clinical symptoms. Knowledge of these various stages and approaches to explore them may be used to assess human nutrient requirements and nutritional status. From Beaton and Patwardham (1973).

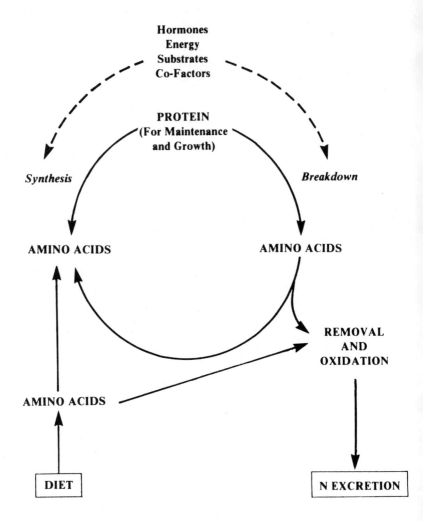

Figure 2: **Protein and Amino Acid Metabolism.**
Body and organ protein content is determined by the balance between the rates of protein synthesis and breakdown, and each of these phases of protein metabolism are influenced by factors including hormones, substrate (amino acids, nitrogen) and energy supply. The recycling of amino acids is a major pathway of whole body amino acid metabolism. From Young and Pellett (1984).

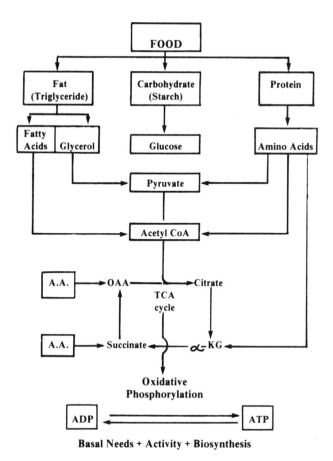

Figure 3: **The Use of Fats, Carbohydrates and Protein as Sources of Energy.**
Additional routes (See Figure 5) between pyruvate, OAA, and PEP allow gluconeogenesis to occur. The metabolism of amino acids is dependent on their individual structure. In an individual TG some 16-20 carbons are in the form of FA to each one in glycerol

AA amino acids, OAA oxaloacetate, KG alpha keto glutarate, ADP adenosine diphosphate, ATP adenosine tripho phate

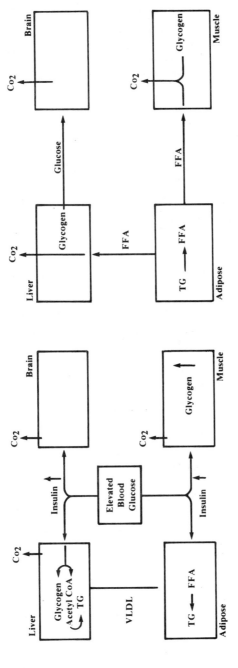

a) Immediately following a meal: Elevated blood glucose causes increases in insulin. This allows uptake of glucose by all tissues where it is either used for energy, stored as glycogen (liver and muscle) or converted to triglyceride (liver and adipose tissue). Although not shown, elevated levels of amino acids and chylomicra would also be used or stored. The former being 'stored' as protein or as glycogen the latter being 'stored' as triglyceride.

b) Five to six hours following a meal: Blood glucose supplies brain and red cell needs. These needs are thus being supplied by liver glycogen. Free fatty acids from adipose tissue supply energy needs for other tissues together with muscle glycogen for muscle needs.

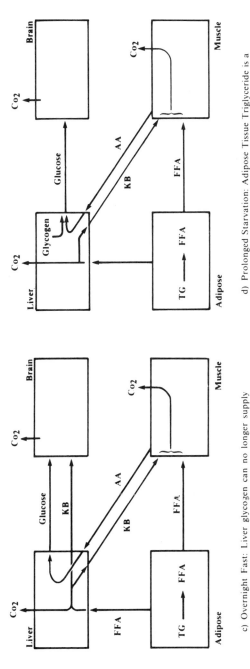

c) Overnight Fast: Liver glycogen can no longer supply sufficient glucose thus becomes supplemented by gluconeogenesis from muscle protein. Ketone body production is initiated in the liver and is used for energy by extra–hepatic tissue but at low levels.

d) Prolonged Starvation: Adipose Tissue Triglyceride is a major source of energy for the body. In the brain, adaptation now allows KB use for energy. Protein conservation occurs and gluconeogenesis from muscle protein is minimized.

Figure 4: **The Biochemical Sequence from Surfeit to Starvation.**

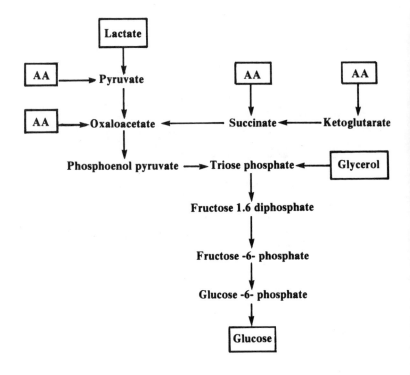

Figure 5: **Routes for Gluconeogenesis from Various Precursors.**
AA Amino Acid(s): The majority, but not all of the protein amino acids can contribute 3 carbons for glucose synthesis. The point at which any amino acid joins the process is dependent on its individual structure.

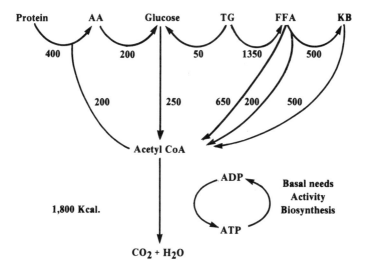

Figure 6: **Utilization of Metabolic Fuels During Fasting.**
Numbers represent Kcal per day by the various routes and total about 1800 Kcal/day. Protein (400 Kcal metabolizable energy) approximates to 16 g N/day loss. Values are for a 3-4 day fast. Adapted from Blackburn and Phinney (1983)

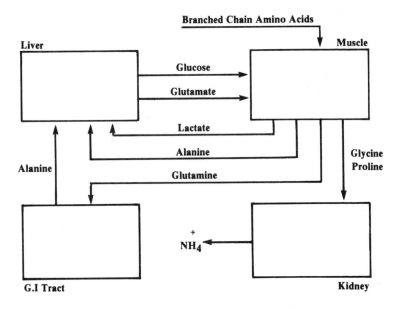

Figure 7: **Cycles of Amino Acid Exchange Between Various Organs in Normal Post-absorptive Man.**

Arterio-venous differences across liver show removal of the glucogenic amino acids, especially alanine and serine, with a net production of glutamate. Glutamine conversion to alanine by the non-hepatic viscera increases the importance of liver alanine uptake. The branched chain amino acids are not utilized by the liver and in certain catabolic states may even be produced. Source; adapted from Cahill, Aoki and Smith (1981).

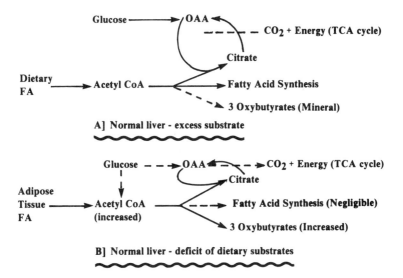

Figure 8: **The Pathways for Ketogenesis.**

    a) when glucose and dietary FA are available fatty acid synthesis will be of major importance.

    b) when adipose tissue FA are mobilized and glucose availability may be limited, acetyl CoA conversion to 3-oxybutyrates is enhanced.

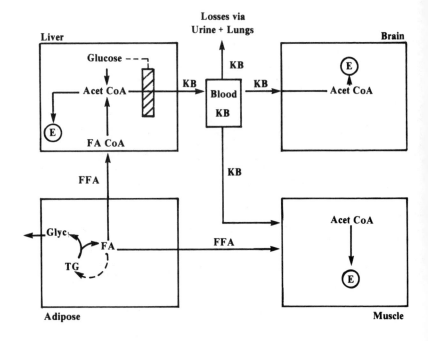

Figure 9: **The Metabolism of Ketone Bodies.**
When adipose tissue is being used as the main fuel supply conversion to KB is enhanced. In the liver, partial oxidation of FFA to KB produces ATP for the cell as well as KB which can be used in extrahepatic tissue. Significant brain use would not occur until starvation was well advanced. KB utilization by tissues would spare glucose and hence muscle. KB also have an important role in acid–base balance. Glucose availability, insulin initiated, can control KB production. The level of KB production is dependent on fat stores.

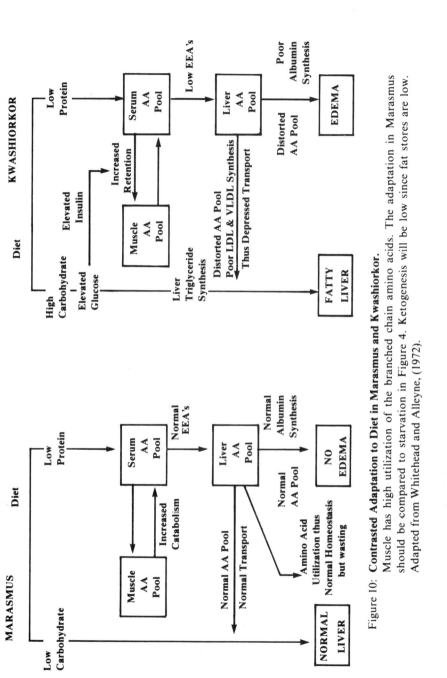

Figure 10: **Contrasted Adaptation to Diet in Marasmus and Kwashiorkor.**
Muscle has high utilization of the branched chain amino acids. The adaptation in Marasmus should be compared to starvation in Figure 4. Ketogenesis will be low since fat stores are low. Adapted from Whitehead and Alleyne, (1972).

# REFERENCES CITED

1984a. Aflotoxins and kwashiorkor. *Nut. Rev.* 42(7):25–26.

1984b. Aflotoxins and kwashiorkor. *The Lancet II:* 1133–1134.

Alamagir, M. 1980. *The dimensions of undernutrition and malnutrition in developing countries: conceptual, empirical and policy issues.* Development discussion paper No. 82. Harvard Institute for International Development. Cambridge, MA: Harvard University.

Alleyne, G.A.O., et al. 1972. Metabolic changes in children with protein-calorie malnutrition. In *Nutrition and development,* ed. M. Winick, 201–238. New York: J. Wiley and Sons.

Alleyne, G.A.O., et al. 1977. *Protein–energy malnutrition.* London: Edward Arnold.

A.I.D. (Agency for International Development). 1978 Arab Republic of Egypt, National Nutrition Survey, U.S. Agency for International Development. Washington, D.C.: U.S. Dept. of State.

Aoki, T.T., et al. 1975. The metabolic effects of glucose in brief and prolonged fasted man. *Am. J. Clin. Nutr.* 28:507–511.

Balagura, S. 1973. *Hunger: A biopsychological analysis.* New York: Basic Books.

Bang, F. B. 1978. The role of disease in the ecology of famine. *Ecol. Fd. Nutr.* 7:1–15.

Beaton, G.H. 1983. Energy in human nutrition: W.O. Atwater Memorial Lecture. *Nutrition Today.* 9/10:6–14. Also 1983 *Nutr. Rev.* 41(11) 325–340.

Beaton, G.H., and V. N. Patwardhan. 1976. Physiological and practical considerations of nutrient function and requirements. In *Nutrition in preventive medicine,* ed. G. H. Beaton and J. M. Bengoa, WHO Monograph Series no. 203. Geneva: World Health Organization.

Benedict, F.G. 1907. The influence of inanition on metabolism. Washington, DC: Carnegie Institute of Washington.

Benedict, F.G. 1915. *A study of prolonged fasting.* Publication no. 203. Washington, DC: Carnegie Institute of Washington.

Benedict, F.G., 1919. *Human vitality and efficiency under prolonged restricted diet.* Publication no. 280. Washington, DC: Carnegie Institute of Washington.

Bengoa, J.M. 1973 State of world malnutrition. In *Man, food and nutrition.* ed. M. Rechcigl, 1–14 Cleveland: CRC Press.

Bengoa, J.M. and G. Donoso. 1974. Prevalence of protein–calorie malnutrition. *PAG Bulletin* 4:24–35.

Biswas, M.R., and A.K. Biswas, eds. 1979. *Food, climate and man.* New York: Wiley.

Blackburn, G.L., and S.D. Phinney. 1983. Lipid metabolism in injury. In J.F. Burke, 98–120.

Blix, G., Y. Hofvander and B. Vahlquist, eds. 1971. Famine: A symposium dealing with nutrition and relief operations in times of disaster. 9th Symposium. Swedish Nutritional Foundation. Uppsala, Sweden: Almqvist and Wiksells.

Bloom, W. L. 1959. Fasting as an introduction to the treatment of obesity. *Metabolism* 8:214–220.

Booth, D.A. ed. 1978. *Hunger models: computable theory of feeding control.* London: Academic Press.

Brand, W. 1980. North–South, a programme for survival. The Report of the Independent Commission on International Development Issues Cambridge, MA: M.I.T. Press.

Brooke, O.G., and A. Ashworth. 1972. The influence of malnutrition on the postprandian metabolic rate and respiratory quotient. *The British Journal of Nutrition.* 27:407–415.

Broquist, H.P., D. W. Horne, and V. Tanphaichitr. 1975. Lysine metabolism in protein–calorie malnutrition with attention to the synthesis of carnitine. In R.E. Olson, 49–63.

Brown, L. R. 1981. World population growth, soil erosion and food security. *Science* 214:995–1002.

Brozek, J. 1982. The impact of malnutrition on behavior. In Nutrition policy implementation: Issues and experience, ed. N.S. Scrimshaw and M. B. Wallerstein, New York: Plenum Press: 21–35.

Burger, G.C.E., J. D. Drummond, and M.R. Sanstead.1948.*Malnutrition and starvation in Western Netherlands 1944-1945.* 2 vols. The Hague: Netherlands General State Printing Press.

Burke, J.F. 1983. *Surgical physiology.* Philadelphia: Saunders.

Cahill, G. F., Jr. 1970. Starvation in man. *New Engl. J. Med.* 282:668–675.

Cahill, G.F., Jr. 1978. Physiology of acute starvation in man. *Ecol. Fd. Nutr.* 6:221–230.

Cahill, G. F., Jr., *et al.* 1966. Hormone fuel interrelationships during fasting. *J. Clin. Invest.* 45:1751-1769.

Cahill, G. F., Jr., T. T. Aoki, and R. J. Smith 1981. Amino acid cycles in man. In *Current topics in cellular regulation.* Vol. 18, ed. R. W. Estabrook and P. Srere, 389–400. New York: Academic Press.

Calloway, D. H. 1977. The functional definition of nutritional status. *PAG Bulletin* 7:53–58.

Cannon, W. B. 1932. *The wisdom of the body.* New York: Norton.

Cerra, F.B., J. H. Siegel, and J. R. Border. 1983. The systemic–metabolic–physiologic response to sepsis. Burke, 169–186.

Chandra, R. K. 1981. Immunocompetence as a functional index of physiologic response to sepsis. *Br. Med. Bull.* 37:39–94.

Chandra, R. K. 1982. Malnutrition and infection. In *Nutrition policy implementation: Issues and experience.* ed. N.S. Scrimshaw and M. B. Wallerstein, 44–51. New York: Plenum Press.

Chen, L. C. 1978. Control of diarrhoeal disease morbidity and mortality: Some strategic issues. *Am. J. Clin. Nutr.* 31: 2284–2291.

Chen L. C. 1983. Planning for the control of the diarrhoea–malnutrition complex. In *Nutrition in the community.* 2d ed. ed. D. S. McLaren, 143-160. Chichester: Wiley.

Chen, L.C. and N. S. Scrimshaw, eds. 1982. *Diarrhea and malnutrition: interactions, mechanisms and interventions.* New York: Plenum Press.

Coward, W.A. and P. G. Lunn. 1981. The biochemistry and physiology of kwashiorkor and marasmus. *Br. Med. Bull. 37:19–24.*

Cox, G. W. 1978. *The ecology of famine: An overview. Ecol. Fd. Nutr.* 6:207–220.

Cravioto, J., L. Hambraeus, and B. Vahlquist, eds. 1974. Early malnutrition and mental development. Uppsala: Almquist and Wiksell.

Currey, B. 1978. The famine syndrome: Its definition for relief and rehabilitation in Bangladesh. *Ecol. Fd. Nutr.* 6:207–220.

Dando, W. A. 1983. Biblical famines 1850 BC–AD46; Insights for modern mankind. *Ecol. Fd. Nutr.* 13:231–249.

Dept. Expt. Medicine. 1951. The German background, studies in undernutrition. Wuppertal, 1946–1949. *Spec. Rep. Ser. Med. Res. Coun.* no. 275. London, 1951.

Douglas, S. D. 1981. Impact of malnutrition on non-specific defense. In Isliker and Schurch, 28–36.

Duncan, G. C., et al. 1962. Correction and control of intractable obesity. *J. Amer. Med. Assoc.* 18:309–312

Durnin, J. V. G. A., and R. Passmore. 1967. Energy, work and leisure. London: Heineman.

Eichler, G. K. 1982. Facing up to Africa's food crisis. *Foreign Affairs* 61:151–174.

Epstein, A. N., H. R. Kissileff, and E. Stellar, eds. 1973. The neuropsychology of thirst: new findings and advances in concepts. Washington: Winston.

FAO. 1946. *World Food Survey.* Washington, D.C.: Food and Agricultural Organization of the United Nations.

FAO. 1952. *Second World Food Survey.* Rome: Food and Agriculture Organization.

FAO. 1957a. *Calorie requirements*. FAO Nutritional Studies, no. 15. Rome: Food and Agriculture Organization.

FAO. 1957b. *Protein requirements*. FAO Nutritional Studies, no. 16. Rome: Food and Agriculture Organization.

FAO. 1963. *Third World Food Survey*. Freedom from Hunger, Basic Study II. Rome: Food and Agriculture Organization.

FAO. 1977. *Fourth World Survey*. Statistics Series no. 11 and Food and Nutrition Series no. 10. Rome: Food and Agriculture Organization.

FAO. 1980. Average and per caput food supplies. *Food Balance Sheets, 1975-1977*. Rome: Food and Agriculture Organization.

FAO. 1981. *Agriculture: Toward 2000*. Rome: Food and Agriculture Organization.

FAO. 1982. *The state of food and agriculture 1981*. Rome: Food and Agriculture Organization.

FAO. 1983. *The state of food and agriculture 1982*. Rome: Food and Agriculture Organization.

FAO/WHO. 1965. *Protein requirements*. FAO nutritional studies no. 16. Rome: Food and Agriculture Organization.

FAO/WHO. 1973. *Energy and protein requirements*. Food and Agriculture Organization nutrition meetings report series no. 52. Rome: Food and Agriculture Organization.

FAO/WHO/UNU. 1985. *Energy and protein requirements*. Report of a Joint FAO/WHO/UNU Meeting. Geneva: World Health Organization.

Feachem, F.G., and M. A. Koblinsky. 1984. Interventions for the control of diarrhoeal diseases among young children: promotion of breast feeding. *Bull Wrld Heth Org. 62/2) 271-291*.

Felig, P. 1973. The glucose–alanine cycle. *Metabolism* 22:179-207.

Felig, P., O. E. Owen, J. Wahren, and G. F. Cahill, Jr. 1969. Amino acid metabolism during prolonged starvation. *J. Clin.Invest.* 48:584-594.

Felig, P., et al. 1970. Alanine: Key role in gluconeogenesis. *Science* 167:1003–1004.

Felig, ., and J. Wahren. 1971. Influence of endogenous insulin secretions on splanchnic glucose and amino acid metabolism in man. *J. Clin. Invest.* 50:1702–1711.

Felig, P., O. E. Owen and G. F. Cahill, Jr. 1971. Metabolic response to human growth hormone during prolonged starvation. *J. Clin. Invest.* 50:411–421.

Flatt, J. P., and G. L. Blackburn. 1974. The metabolic fuel regulatory system: Implications for protein sparing therapy during caloric deprivation or disease. *Am. J. Clin. Nutr.*27:175–187.

Foege, W. H. 1971. Famine, infections and epidemics. In Blix, et al., 65–72.

Garber, A. J., P. H. Menzel, G. Boden, and O. E. Owen. 1974. Hepatic ketogenesis and gluconeogenesis in humans. *J. Clin. Invest.* 54:981–989.

Garrow, J. S. 1974. *Energy balance and obesity in man.* New York: Elsevier.

Garrow, J. S. and S. Blaza. 1982. Energy requirements in human beings. In *Human nutrition:* Current issues and controversies. eds. A. Neuberger and T. H. Jukes, 1–21. Lancaster, U. K.: MTP Press.

Garza, C., N. S. Scrimshaw, and V. R. Young. 1977. Human protein requirements: A long term metabolic nitrogen balance study in young men to evaluate the 1973 FAO/WHO safe level of egg protein intake. *J.Nutr.* 107:335–352.

George, S. 1975. *How the other half dies; The real reasons for world hunger.* Harmondsworth, U.K.: Penguin.

Golden, M.H.N. *et al.* 1978. Zinc and immunocompetence in protein-energy malnutrition. *Lancet* 1:1226–1228.

Grande, F. 1968. Energetics and weight reduction. *Am. J. Clin. Nutr.* 21:305–314.

Griffey-Brechin, S.J. 1984. The etiology of low birth weight and its economic impact in developing countries. *Ecol. Fd. Nutr.* 21:325–335.

Gross, R.L. and P. M. Newberne. 1980. Role of nutrition in immunologic function. *Physiol. Rev.* 60:188-302.

Hansen, M. A., G. Fernandes and R. A. Good. 1982. Nutrition and immunity: The influence of diet on autoimmunity and the role of zinc in the immune response. *Ann. Rev. Nutr.* 2:151-177.

Harfouche, J. K. 1979. Health care problems of the young child in a developing context. *Bull. Wld. Hlth. Org.* 57(3):387-403.

Harris, J.A. and F. G. Benedict. 1919. *A biometric study of basal metabolism in man.* Pub. no. 279. Washington, D.C.: Carnegie Institute.

Hendrickse, R.G., *et al.* 1982. Aflotoxins and kwashiorkor: A study in Sudanese children. *Br. Med. J.* 285:843-846.

Isliker, H., and B. Schurch, eds. 1981. *The impact of malnutrition on immune defense in parasitic infestation. A Nestle Foundation workshop.* Berne: Hans Huber.

Jelliffe, D.B. 1959. Protein-calorie malnutrition in tropical pre-school children: A review of recent knowledge. *J. Pediat.* 54:227-256.

Kallen, D. J., ed. 1973. *Nutrition, development and social behavior.* Washington, D.C.: GPO.

Keys, A. J., *et al.* 1950. *The biology of human starvation. 2 vols.* Minneapolis: University of Minnesota Press.

Kleiber, M. 1961. *The fire of life: an introduction to animal energetics.* New York: Wiley.

Knack, A. V., and J. Neuman. 1917. See Keys, et al.

Kohn, K. 1920. See Keys, et al.

Lappe, F. M., and J. Collins. 1977. *Food first; Beyond the myth of scarcity.* Boston, Houghton Mifflin.

Latham, M. C. 1975. Nutrition and infection in national development. *Science* 188:561-565.

Latham, M. C. 1979. *Human nutrition in tropical Africa.* Food and Nutrition Series, no 11, rev. 1. Rome: FAO.

Lechtig, A., et al. 1979. Effects of maternal nutrition on the mother-child dyad. In *The Mother-Child dyad: Nutritional aspects.* ed. L. Hambraeus and S. Sjolin. Stockholm: Almqvist and Wiksell International.

Levenson, S. M., and E. Seifter. 1983. *Starvation: Metabolic and physiologic responses.* In Burke, 121–168.

McGilvery, R. W. 1982. *Biochemistry: A functional approach.* 2d ed. Philadelphia: W. B. Saunders.

McKigney, J. I. 1985. Vitamin A deficiency: Signs, symptoms, and solutions. *Horizons* 4(1);24–27.

McLaren, D. C. 1983. Nutrition policy, planning and programmes: A personal overview. In McLaren, ed., 1–16.

McLaren, D. S., ed. 1983. *Nutrition in the community: a critical look at nutrition policy planning and programmes.* 2d. ed. Chichester: Wiley.

McLaren, D. S., and P. L. Pellett. 1970. Nutrition in the Middle East. *World Rev. Nutr. Dietet.* 12:43–127.

McLaren, D. S., P. L. Pellett, and W. W. Read. 1967. A simple scoring system for classifying the severe forms of protein–calorie malnutrition of early childhood. *Lancet* I:533–537.

Maletnlena, T. N. 1980. How Europe can contribute to nutrition research for developing countries. In Hambraeus, ed. *Nutrition in Europe.* Stockholm: Almqvist and Wiksell, 10–15.

Marliss, E. B., et al. 1970. Glucagon levels and metabolic effects in fasting man. *J. Clin. Invest.* 49:2256–2270.

Marliss, E. B., et al. 1971. Muscle and splanchnic glutamine and glutamate metabolism in post absorptive and starved man. *J. Clin. Invest.* 50:814–817.

Mason, J. B., et al. 1984. *Nutritional surveillance.* Geneva; WHO.

Mata, L. J., and M. Behar. 1975. Malnutrition and infection in a typical rural Guatamalan village: Lessons for the planning of preventative measures. *Ecol. Fd. Nutr.* 4:41–47.

Mayer, J. 1985. Preventing Famine. *Science* 227:707.

Novin, D., W. Wyricka, and G. A. Bray, eds. 1976. *Hunger: Basic mechanisms and clinical implications.* New York: Raven.

Olson, R. E., ed. 1975. *Protein-calorie malnutrition.* New York: Academic Press.

Omalulu, A., M. A. Hussain, and C. F. Mbofung. 1981. A transverse-longitudional study of heights and weights of children in a Nigerian village. *Nigerian J. Paediatrics* 8:(3):70–78.

Owen, O. E., et al. 1969. Liver and kidney metabolism during prolonged starvation. *J. Clin. Invest.* 48:574–594.

Owen, O. E., and G. A. Reichard. 1971. Human forearm metabolism during progressive starvation. *J. Clin. Invest.* 50:1536– 1545.

Owen, O. E., et al. 1978. Interrelationships among key tissues and the utilization of metabolic substrates. In Katzen and Mahler, eds. *Diabetes, obesity, and vascular disease.* New York: Wiley.

Owen, O. E., et al. 1979. Energy metabolism in feasting and fasting. *Adv. Expt. Med. Biol.* III:169–188.

Pellett, P. L. 1983. Changing concepts on world malnutrition. *Ecol. Fd. Nutr.* 13:115–125.

Pellett, P.L. 1985. In press. Problems and pitfalls in the assessment of nutritional status. In M. Harris, ed. *Food preferences and aversions.* Wenner Gren Foundation for Anthropological Research Symposium, 1983.

Pellett, P. L., and V. R. Young, eds. 1980. *Nutritional evaluation of protein foods.* Food and Nutrition Bulletin Supplement no. 4. Tokyo; United Nations University. WHTR3/ UNUP 129.

Peters, G., J. T. Fitzsimons, and L. Peters-Haefeli. 1975. *Control mechanisms of drinking.* New York: Springer Verlag.

Pinstrup-Andersen, P. 1983. Estimating the nutritional impact of food policies: A note on the analytical approach. *Food Nutr. Bull.* 5(4):16–21.

Poleman, T. T. 1981a. Quantifying the nutrition situation in developing countries. *Food Res. Inst. Stud.* XVIII(1),1–58.

Poleman, T. T. 1981b. A reappraisal of the extent of world hunger. *Food Policy* 6(4):236–252.

Porter, A. 1950. *The diseases of the Madras Famine of 1877–78.* Madras: Government Press. Cited by Keys, et al., 1950.

Puffer, R. R., and C. V. Serrano. 1973. *Patterns of mortality in childhood.* Report of the Inter-American investigation of mortality in childhood. Pan American Health Organization Scientific publication no. 262. Washington, DC: PAHO.

Rand, W. M., and N. S. Scrimshaw. 1984. Protein and energy requirements: Insights from long-term studies. *NFI Bulletin (Nutrition Foundation of India) October: 5(4).*

Rand, W. M., R. Uauay, and N. S. Scrimshaw. 1984. *Protein-energy-requirement studies in developing countries: Results of international research.* Food and Nutrition Bulletin Supplement 10 WHTR-8/UNUP 481. Tokyo: United Nations University.

Reutlinger, S., and M. Selowsky 1976. *Malnutrition and poverty; Magnitude and policy options.* World Bank Staff Occasional Paper no. 23. Baltimore: Johns Hopkins University Press.

Rolls, B. J., and E. T. Rolls. 1982. *Thirst.* Cambridge: Cambridge University Press.

Sai, F. T. 1984. The population factor in Africa's development dilemma. *Science* 226:801–805.

Sampson, D. A., and G. R. Jansen. 1984. Protein and energy nutrition during lactation. *Ann. Rev. Nutrition.* 4:43–67.

Schuftan, C. 1983. Ethics and ideology in the battle against malnutrition. In McLaren, D. S., 125–141.

Scrimshaw, N. S. 1975. Interactions of malnutrition and infection: Advances in understanding. In *Protein-calorie malnutrition,* ed. R. E. Olson, 353–367. New York: Academic Press.

Scrimshaw, N. S., C. E. Taylor, and J. E. Gordon. 1968. *Interactions of nutrition and infection.* WHO Monograph no. 57. Geneva: WHO.

Scrimshaw, N. S., and J. E. Gordon, eds. 1968. *Malnutrition, learning, and behavior.* Cambridge, MA: MIT Press.

Scrimshaw, N. S., et al. 1972. Protein requirements of man: Variations in obligatory and fecal nitrogen losses in young men. *J. Nutr.* 102:1595–1604.

Solomons, N. W. 1985. Rehabilitating the severely malnourished infant and child. *J. Am. Diet. Assoc.* 85(1):28–36.

Solomons, N. W., and L. M. Allen. 1983. The functional assessment of nutritional status: Principles, practice, and potential. *Nutr. Revs.* 41:33–50.

Sommer, A., et al. 1982. Scale of blinding malnutrition. *World Health Forum* 3(1):107–108.

Stein, J., and M. Ferigstein. 1946. Anatomie pathologique de la maladie de famine. *In Maladie de famine.* ed. E. Apfelbaum. Cited by Keys, et al., 1950.

Stumpf, S. E. 1981. The moral dimension of the world's food supply. *Ann. Rev. Nutr.* 1:1–25.

Sukhatme, P. V., and S. Margen. 1982. Autoregulatory homeostatic nature of energy balance. *Am. J. Clin. Nutr.* 35:355–365.

Torun, B., V. R. Young, and W. M. Rand, eds. 1981. *Protein-energy requirements of developing countries: Evaluation of new data.* WHTR–4/UNUP–295. Tokyo: UNU.

Torun, B , and F. E. Viteri. 1984. Protein–energy malnutrition. *In Tropical and geographic medicine,* 984–997. New York: McGraw, Hill,

Truswell, A. S. 1975. Carbohydrate and lipid metabolism in protein-calorie malnutrition. In R. E. Olsen, 1975, 119–141.

Underwood, B. H. 1978. Hypovitaminosis A and its control. *Bull. World. Hlth. Rg.* 56:525–541.

UNICEF. 1984. *The state of world's children.* New York: Oxford University Press for UNICEF.

USDA. 1961. *The world food budget 1962 and 1966.* Foreign Agricultural Economic Report no. 4. Washington, DC: Economic Research Service.

USDA. 1964. *The world food budget 1970.* Foreign Agricultural Economic Report no. 19. Washington, DC: Economic Research Service.

UNU. 1982. The United Nations University Theme III; Hunger, poverty, resources, and the environment. *The United Nations University Newsletter 6(1):3.*

Viteri, F. E. 1976. Definition of the nutrition problem in the labor force. In *Nutrition and agricultural development: Significance and potential for the tropics,* ed. N. S. Scrimshaw and M. Behar, 87-98. New York: Plenum Press.

Viteri, F., R. Whitehead, and V. R. Young, eds. 1979. *Protein-energy requirements under conditions prevailing in developing countries: Current knowledge and research needs.* WHTR-1/UNUP-18. Tokyo: UNU.

Waterlow, J. C. 1975. Adaptation to low protein diets. *In R. E. Olson,* 1975, 23-35.

Waterlow, J. C. 1984. Kwashiorkor revisited: the pathogenesis of oedema in kwashiorkor and its significance. *Trans. Roy. Soc. Trop. Med.* 78:436-41.

Waterlow, J. C., and G. A. O. Alleyne. 1971. Protein malnutrition in children: Advances in knowledge in the last ten years. In *Advances in protein chemistry, vol. 25,* C. B. Anfinsen, J. T. Edsall, and F. M. Richards, eds., 117-141.

Waterlow, J. C., *et al.* 1977. The presentation and use of height and weight data for comparing the nutritional status of groups of children under the age of 10 years. *Bull. World Hlth. Org.* 55:489-498.

Waterlow, J. C., P. J. Garlick, and D. J. Millward. 1978. *Protein turnover in mammalian tissues and in the whole body.* Amsterdam: North Holland.

Wershow, H. J. 1975. A social scientists'counsel on nutrition and mental development. *Ecol. Fd. Nutr.* 4:49-52.

Whitehead, R. 1981. Infection and how it influences the pathogenesis of protein-energy malnutrition. In Isliker and Schurch, 1981, 15–25.

Whitehead, R. G., ed. 1983. *Maternal diet, breast-feeding capacity, and lactational infertility.* WHTR-5/UNUP-338. Tokyo: UNU University

Whitehead, R. G., and G. A. O. Alleyne. 1972. Pathophysiological factors of importance in protein-calorie malnutrition. *Br. Med. Bull.* 28:72–78.

WHO. 1973. *Food and nutrition terminology.* Terminology Circular no. 27.

WHO. 1976. *Vitamin A deficiency and xeropthalmia: Report on a joint WHO/ USAID meeting.* WHO Technical Report Series, no. 590. Geneva: WHO.

WHO. 1980a. *Sixth report on the world health situation, Part I: Global analysis, 290.* Geneva: WHO

WHO. 1980b. Division of Family Health. The incidence of low birth weight: A critical review of available information. *World Health Statistics Quarterly.* 33(3):197–204.

WHO. 1981. *Guidelines for training community health workers in nutrition.* Pub. no. 59. Geneva: WHO.

Wolf, A. V. 1958. *Thirst.* Springfield, IL: Charles C. Thomas.

Woodham-Smith, C. 1962. *The great hunger: Ireland 1845–1849.* New York: Harper and Row.

Young, V. R., and N. S. Scrimshaw. 1973. The physiology of starvation. In Food: Readings from Scientific American. Comp J. H. Hoff and J. Janick, 44–51. San Francisco: Freeman.

Young, V. R., and N. S. Scrimshaw. 1978. Nutritional evaluation of protein and protein requirements. In *Protein sources and technology: Status and research needs.* ed. M. Milner, N. S. Scrimshaw, and D.I.C. Wang, Westport, CT: AVI, 126–173.

Young, V. R., and P. L. Pellett. 1983. Some general consideration of amino acid and protein metabolism and nutrition. In *Surgical physiology.* ed. J. F. Burke, 51–74. Philadelphia: Saunders.

Young, V. R., and P. L. Pellett. 1984. *Milk proteins with reference to human protein needs and the world food and nutrition situation.* Symposium Proceedings in press. Luxembourg: International Congress on Milk Proteins.

Young, V. R., *et al.* 1984. Mechanisms of adaption to protein malnutrition. In K. L. Blaxter and J. C. Waterlow, eds. *Nutritional adaptation in man.* London: John Libbey.

# REDUCING WORLD HUNGER: AN ECONOMIST'S VIEW

## D. Gale Johnson

It is not easy to know what is a reasonable perspective on either the current food situation of the poorer people of the world or what the prospects may be for the future. It is not only that we have been confronted in recent months with the pictures of the horrible conditions in the camps in Ethiopia, with rather little indication of why those conditions prevail. Large relief efforts are underway, but it is not known how much of the food and other relief supplies are reaching those who need them nor what the reasons may be why at least some of the supplies have not left the port areas. But we are also exposed to a wide diversity of views about what the prospects are for improvements in the nutritional status of the world's poor people in the years ahead, either generally or in Africa in particular.

It is true that pessimistic views concerning the future of world food supplies have been put forward several times in the past two decades and such pessimistic views have received much more attention in the press than what might be called more balanced views. By more balanced views, I mean views that have been consistent with the modest improvements in food availability that have occurred over the past three decades. These improvements have benefited the majority of the world's poor people, and I shall present evidence later to support this conclusion.

The attention that has been given to the apparently deteriorating food situation in some parts of Africa may lead some to fear that the recent improvements in food production per capita in Latin America and Asia may not be maintained. There are not adequate grounds for assuming that what has been occurring in Africa in recent years portends a similar result elsewhere in the rest of the developing world. To so argue means to ignore the overwhelming body of evidence that explains why per capita food production in Africa has been gradually declining for the past 15 years (and why the same indicator has been generally increasing in the remainder of the developing countries).

There is no truth to the argument that the primary cause of the current sad African situation has been adverse weather and thus unavoidable. The roots go back many years before the onset of the shortfall of rain of the past two to four years. It is all too easy and common to blame weather for events that result from the actions of man. The adequacy of food supply is far more due to the mix of policies that governments follow than to the availability of natural resources or the vagaries of weather.

## Improvements in Food Supplies

The direct evidence on the adequacy of food supplies and of changes in per capita food supplies is less accurate than one might wish. The poorer the country, the more likely that any measure of food supply will be subject to significant error. Fortunately, in most though perhaps not all instances, the errors will tend to underestimate the availability of food. The reason for this is that in the very poorest economies a part of the food supply comes from "unconventional" sources—foods that are locally produced and consumed and thus may escape being estimated. On the other side, waste and loss in the poorest economies may be rather large and might also be underestimated. I make these comments for two reasons. The first is that while data on per capita food supplies provided by such organizations as the Food and Agriculture Organization or the U.S. Department of Agriculture represent the best available data and have no conscious bias, the trends should be interpreted with some caution. The second is that one should look for other types of evidence that reflect, directly or indirectly, the state of nutrition and health. The following sections present data on the trends in production and food supplies per capita and on other indices of the adequacy of nutrition.

## Recent Trends in Per Capita Food Production

It is well to start our discussion with the available evidence on changes in per capita food production in the developing countries. Recent emphasis on the poor performance of food production in Africa may have left many with the impression that the performance in other developing regions had been no different. As the data in Table 1 indicates, such is not the case. It is the African experience that is unique; in all of the other developing regions there has been steady, if unspectacular, improvement in per capita food production over the past two decades.

The emphasis given to the decline in per capita food production in most African countries should not be interpreted to mean that, in general, total food production has fallen. It is true that food output growth in Africa has been significantly slower than in Asia or Latin America, but growth has occurred. The growth of food production, however, has been slower than the growth of population for Africa as a whole. Crude birth rates are high and have hardly started to decline, while death rates have dropped over the past two decades, generally by 25 percent or more (World Bank 1985).

TABLE 1

ESTIMATED INDEXES OF FOOD PRODUCTION PER CAPITA
FOR DEVELOPING MARKET ECONOMIES BY REGIONS, 1966-84
(1961-65 = 100)

| | Africa | Latin America | Near East[a] | Far East[b] |
|------|--------|---------------|--------------|-------------|
| 1966 | 96 | 101 | 101 | 94 |
| 1967 | 98 | 104 | 103 | 97 |
| 1968 | 100 | 103 | 103 | 101 |
| 1969 | 100 | 104 | 103 | 103 |
| 1970 | 100 | 106 | 103 | 105 |
| 1971 | 99 | 103 | 103 | 103 |
| 1972 | 95 | 101 | 107 | 97 |
| 1973 | 89 | 101 | 99 | 104 |
| 1974 | 93 | 103 | 105 | 99 |
| 1975 | 93 | 103 | 109 | 106 |
| 1976 | 94 | 108 | 111 | 105 |
| 1977 | 87 | 107 | 105 | 106 |
| 1978 | 88 | 110 | 110 | 113 |
| 1979 | 87 | 111 | 107 | 109 |
| 1980 | 87 | 112 | 107 | 110 |
| 1981 | 86 | 113 | 108 | 115 |
| 1982 | 86 | 113 | 108 | 112 |
| 1983 | 80 | 110 | 106 | 118 |
| 1984 | 81 | 110 | 106 | 118 |

Source: FAO, *FAO Production Yearbook,* various issues
[a]The Near East includes Northern Africa and the Middle East.
[b]The Far East includes South, Southeast and East Asia

**Per Capita Food Supplies**

Food production, by itself, does not fully determine the amount of food available for consumption. Consumption is determined by production, change in stocks and net trade in food commodities. If there is sufficient change in the amount of net food trade, a decline in per capita food production need not result in a decline in per capita food supplies. For most developing countries we do not have adequate data on changes in stocks on which to base any estimate of per capita food consumption.

For many developing countries there have been significant shifts in net trade in food that have permitted either offsetting a decline in per capita food production or making possible a significant increase in per capita food supplies when per capita food production has increased quite modestly. As Table 2 indicates, per capita food supplies in developing market economies in Africa have increased slightly since 1961-63. The shift in net trade in food more than offset the decline in per capita food production. Generally speaking, the shifts in net food trade had a significant positive effect on per capita food supplies (measured in calories) in the developing countries.

TABLE 2

PER CAPITA DAILY CALORIE SUPPLY, WORLD AND REGIONS:
1961—63, 1969—71, 1979—81

| | Calories Per Capita Daily | | |
|---|---|---|---|
| Region/Group | 1961—63 | 1969—71 | 1979—81 |
| Developed Countries | 3110 | 3280 | 3380 |
| Developed market economies | 3080 | 3260 | 3370 |
| N. America | 3270 | 3480 | 3610 |
| W. Europe | 3140 | 3290 | 3430 |
| Oceania | 3190 | 3280 | 3150 |
| Other developed | 2540 | 2770 | 2870 |
| Eastern Europe and U.S.S.R. | 3160 | 3320 | 3390 |
| Developing countries | 2000 | 2140 | 2350 |
| Developing market economies | 2080 | 2170 | 2330 |
| Africa | 2130 | 2180 | 2260 |
| Latin America | 2380 | 2510 | 2630 |
| Near East | 2290 | 2410 | 2840 |
| Far East | 1950 | 2030 | 2170 |
| Other developing | 1950 | 2190 | 2310 |
| Asian centrally planned economies | 1840 | 2080 | 2410 |
| World | 2350 | 2470 | 2620 |

Source: Mollett (1985, Table 1, p. 28).

The estimated per capita calorie supply for Africa in 1979-81 was 2,260 or 130 calories greater than in 1961-63. In 1961-63 Africa was a net food exporter. In those years, its exports of food in terms of calories was about 5 percent of its food consumption; by 1969-71 net exports of food had declined to 1 percent of food consumption. But in the next decade food imports increased sharply, and by 1979-81, 16 percent of total food supplies were imported (Mollett 1985). Thus the trade changes in two decades made possible an increase in daily calorie consumption of about 20 percent compared to the decline of per capita food production of about 10 percent. Without such a change in consumption due to food imports, the current African food situation would be far more disastrous than it is.

**Other Evidence[1]**

The data on food supplies per capita are only approximate indicators of changes in nutritional status. The data on food availability are for entire populations and we have very little information about the distribution among or within families of actual food consumption. However, we have data on vital statistics—life expectancy, infant mortality, child mortality—that provide some evidence on changes in nutritional status. Robert Fogel has brought together a large amount of relevant evidence on the relationships between nutrition and the decline in mortality over the past three centuries. While much of the evidence is for the countries of Western Europe and North America, some data are from the Caribbean low income areas. Using data on average adult stature as a measure of nutritional status, the preliminary conclusion is "Improvements in nutritional status may have accounted for as much as four tenths of the decline in mortality rates, but nearly all of this effect was concentrated in the reduction of infant mortality." Life expectancy at birth in England at the beginning of the 18th Century was 35 years, approximately the same as in the low income countries in 1950.

The data in Table 3 are quite striking and are fully consistent with the conclusion that there has been significant improvement in health and nutritional status among the world's poor people. For the developing countries as a group, the largest absolute increase in life expectancy at birth between 1960 and 1982 was for the lowest income countries—an increase from 42 years in 1960 to 59 years in 1982. The increase of 17 years may well be distorted by the large increase in China (indicated separately in the table). But note that for the lowest income countries in Africa that life expectancy increased by 10 years to 48 years in 1982. India, with a low per capita gross national product of $260 per capita, had a life expectancy of 55 years in 1982, an increase of 12 years in little more than a decade.

A life expectancy of 55 to 60 years may not seem so very long to those of you who think of the life expectancy of 75 years now achieved in the United States, Western Europe and Japan. But persons born as recently as 1920 in the United States had an expected life span of 55 years, a figure now equaled by India, Burma and Haiti—three of the poorest countries in the world—and exceeded by a decade or more in Brazil, Mexico and South Korea.

The large declines in infant and child mortality have made a major contribution to the recent increases in life expectancy in low income countries. Between 1960 and 1982 for the developing countries with per capita incomes of less than $390 infant mortality was reduced by almost half—from 165 per thousand births to 87 per thousand births. The decline in African low income countries was less, from 164 to 117. It is worth noting

TABLE 3

LIFE EXPECTANCY AT BIRTH, INFANT MORTALITY RATES AND CHILD DEATH RATE: AFRICA, 1960 AND 1982

| Country Group | Life Expectancy at Birth | | Infant Mortality Rate ( < 1) | | Child Death Rate (ages 1—4) | | GNP Per Capita |
|---|---|---|---|---|---|---|---|
| | 1960 | 1982 | 1960 | 1982 | 1960 | 1982 | 1982 ($) |
| Africa | | | | | | | |
| Low income: | | | | | | | |
| Semi-arid | 37 | 44 | 203 | 151 | 57 | 34 | 218 |
| Other | 39 | 49 | 158 | 112 | 37 | 22 | 254 |
| Average | 38 | 48 | 164 | 117 | 40 | 24 | 249 |
| Middle income: | | | | | | | |
| Oil importers | 41 | 50 | 159 | 111 | 37 | 21 | 670 |
| Oil exporters | 39 | 50 | 191 | 113 | 51 | 21 | 889 |
| Sub-Saharan Africa | — | 49 | 170 | 115 | 42 | 23 | 491 |
| Low-income Economies: | | | | | | | |
| China | 42 | 67 | 165 | 67 | 26 | 7 | 310 |
| India | 43 | 55 | 165 | 94 | 26 | 11 | 260 |
| All other | 43 | 51 | 163 | 114 | | | 250 |
| Average | 42 | 59 | 165 | 87 | | | 280 |
| Middle-income Economies | 51 | 62 | 126 | 76 | 23 | 10 | 1,520 |
| Lower-middle income | 46 | 57 | 144 | 89 | 29 | 13 | 840 |
| Upper-middle income | 56 | 65 | 101 | 58 | 15 | 6 | 2,490 |
| Industrial Market Economies | 70 | 75 | 29 | 10 | 2 | — | 11,070 |
| Developing Countries by 1982 Per Capita Income: | | | | | | | |
| Less than $390 | 42 | 59 | 165 | 87 | 27 | 11 | 280 |
| Excluding China | 42 | 53 | | | | | |
| $440—$1,610 | 50 | 60 | 144 | 89 | 29 | 13 | 840 |
| $1,680—$6,840 | 56 | 65 | 101 | 58 | 15 | 6 | 2,490 |

Source: World Bank, *World Development Report 1984.*

that in 1960 infant mortality rates in the low income countries of Africa were the same as in the remaining low income countries of the world. However, the more modest improvements in food supplies and in incomes generally in Africa than in other low income countries was probably responsible for the more modest reduction in infant mortality. But even though the reduction in infant mortality in Africa was less than elsewhere, it was still a reduction of approximately a third in two decades. For comparison with Africa and the other low income countries, it may be noted that in the U.S. infant mortality in 1900 was 160 and declined by half by 1920. Countries with less than $390 income per capita now have approximately the same infant mortality rate as the United States did in 1920 and achieved that rate with a much lower level of per capita income than the U.S. had in 1920. The child death rate has also declined, generally at a more rapid rate than the infant mortality rate.

## Some Recent Projections

I have not made projections of the amounts of agricultural products that would be produced, consumed or traded for the rest of this century. My views concerning the future trends of supply and demand are based on somewhat impressionistic analyses of past trends of certain critical variables, especially real prices as related to underlying trends in consumption, production, trade and measures of productivity of agricultural resources.

I am not opposed to such projections. In fact, I believe that the types of projections presented in *The Global 2000 Report to the President* (Barney) or in *Agriculture: Toward 2000* (FAO 1981) are of significant value, if properly understood and analyzed. Each of the sets of projections are consistent with the view that world supply will grow at least as fast as food demand for the rest of this century and, consequently, that real food prices will be stationary or declining. Furthermore, the least robust of the projections in each exercise indicated an increase in availability of food per capita in the low-income or developing areas.

The fact that both sets of projections were interpreted differently and in primarily negative terms is largely beside the point. As Fred Sanderson, of Resources for the Future (RFF), has noted both *Global 2000* and *Agriculture: Toward 2000* were political documents, and the startling conclusions presented either in the reports or attributed by others to the reports are unreasonable interpretations of the underlying projections of supply and demand and productivity growth. In comparing the projections from these two reports with projections recently completed for RFF, Sanderson said: "Surprisingly, these differences in slant or tone cannot be explained by significant differences in the basic projections."

While *Global 2000* has left most of its readers with great pessimism concerning the prospective food supplies for the world's poor people, the specific projections of supply and demand growth support moderately optimistic outlooks. For example, the following sentence was italicized in the report:

> The world has the capacity, both physical
> and economic, to produce enough food to
> meet substantial increases in demand
> through 2000 (p.77).

The text goes on to note that the projections of *Global 2000* are "compatible in this regard with a number of other studies suggesting a world food potential several times higher than current production levels. The food growth rates implied in this study's production and consumption projections are comparable to the record increases reported for the 1950's and 1960's." Earlier (page 17) it was noted that the projections indicate an increase in per capita food consumption of 9 percent for 1970 to 2000 for the low income developing countries (LDC) as a whole. It is then pointed out, quite correctly in my opinion, that this gain would not be equally distributed among the LDCs. In particular Africa was singled out as an area where per capita consumption might fall, though as noted here, with one third of the period gone there has not yet been an actual decline in calories per capita in Africa. But per capita food production has declined, as *Global 2000* projected. At one point it was stated that for the populous countries of South Asia, with populations of 1.3 billion in the year 2000, food consumption would "hardly improve at all . . . " Yet on the same page (page 17) it was projected that in this region the average caloric intake would increase slightly—from 12 percent below the FAO standard in the mid-1970's to about 3 percent below the standard in the year 2000. Is an increase of 10 percent "slight"? I would hazard the guess that the poorer people of India, Pakistan and Bangladesh would not so describe an increase of 200 to 225 calories per day per capita as slight, but would rather view it as a significant and welcome improvement in the quality of their lives.

*Agriculture: Toward 2000,* the FAO publication, included projections of the prospective demand and supply for food, with special emphasis upon grains, for 90 developing countries (excluding China). It was noted that a continuation of recent trends in production and demand worldwide "implies large global surpluses in some commodities, despite the growing millions of seriously undernourished, and deficits in other, mainly livestock products." With respect to grains, the net surplus of almost 50 million tons would result by 2000 if recent trends were maintained. The net availabilities from developing countries of "such competing products as sugar, citrus fruit and vegetable oils and oilseeds would substantially outstrip import demand in the developed countries, whose protectionism would limit severely any expansion in their imports of these products." It was then added that the surpluses would not actually occur since either price or policy-induced adjustments would bring about an approximate balance between world supply and demand. But the main point was that except for livestock products the pressure of supply and demand developments would be to put downward, *not* upward, pressure on prices.

The most optimistic aspect of the FAO report consists of the outlines of feasible alternatives to the trend projections. Either of the major alternatives, if realized, would permit significant further improvement in income growth, agricultural output, per capita food supplies, a reduction in cereal imports and an increase in the net surplus in agricultural trade for the 90 developing countries. The two scenarios that were developed indicate that annual agricultural output growth rates for the low income developing countries could be increased from the 2.7 percent to 3.1 to 3.8 percent (FAO 1981). For the 41 low income developing countries the scenario that could result in a 3.1 percent annual growth of agricultural production would provide an increase in calories sufficient to increase per capita consumption from 95 percent of average requirements for 1974–76 to 109 percent in 2000; if agricultural output grew at the trend rate of 3.8 percent, there would be significant nutritional improvement and caloric intake would reach 115 percent of average requirement (Table 7, FAO 1981).

The quotation from *Agriculture: Toward 2000* included the phrase "despite the growing millions of seriously undernourished . . . " This phrase brings up the point of what constitutes an improvement in nutritional status, and understanding that point helps to explain why different individuals may evaluate the same trends rather differently. The population of the 90 developing countries will grow significantly by 2000—by about 60 percent between 1980 and 2000 to a total population of 3.63 billion. The Food and Agricultural Organization of the United Nations (FAO) is measuring progress in reducing malnutrition in terms of the absolute number who are malnourished rather than in terms of the percentage of a population that is malnourished.

With a population that has some number of people who are malnourished and growing at about 2.4 percent annually, to hold constant the absolute number of persons malnourished requires that the percentage of the population malnourished decline at the same rate as population grows. This is a rather stringent criterion but perhaps not an impossible one. The report presents trend projections and two alternative scenarios, briefly described above. I believe the results of the trend projections and the two scenarios can be readily interpreted to indicate that the resources—natural and human—exist to provide for a significant improvement in the nutritional status for the vast majority of the population of the developing countries. Even with the trend projections of agricultural production and incomes, the percentage of the population of the developing countries (excluding China) classified as "seriously malnourished" would decline from 23 percent to 17 percent (FAO, 1981. Table 7). However, with the scenario providing for modest improvement over trend, the percentage malnourished in 2000 would decline to 11 percent and with the more optimistic scenario the decline would be to 7 percent. In each of the two alternative scenarios, the absolute number of seriously malnourished would decline. But, in my opinion, a reduction in the percentage malnourished from 23 to 17 percent, assuming the trend projections are realized, represents an important improvement in the nutritional status of the populations of the developing countries.

A recent projection of food supply and demand to the year 2000 has been made by Resources for the Future in cooperation with Economic Perspectives, Inc. (Sanderson 1984a and 1984b). The projections cover 1980–2000 and a deliberate effort was made to avoid giving weight to the effects of the world recession of the early 1980's upon slowing demand growth and the accumulation of large stocks during those years (Sanderson). It has been all too common to project into the future the trends of a very short period, such as 1972–74 or 1967–69, and proclaim either short supplies with sharply rising food prices or permanent surpluses with falling food prices.

Projections were made of demand and production growth for twelve regions and for four major groups of food—meat, milk, cereals and oilseeds as well as for cotton. Demand growth was projected by using the per capita income growth and population growth projections of the World Bank for 1980–2000 and income elasticities of demand for each commodity and region. The projected annual growth rates for the food groups by regions for 1978–80 to 2000 are compared to the actual growth rates for the 1970's in Table 4.

These projections indicate a sharp slowdown in growth of demand for cereals, oilseeds and meat with only a modest decline for milk. The slowdown in demand growth results from reduced rates of population growth (except for Sub–Saharan Africa), slower income growth, and declining income elasticities of demand for food. The latter factor is particularly important for meat in many high income countries, where it appears that meat consumption has approached a maximum per capita level and will not respond to further increases in per capita income.

Production projections were also made by commodity groups and regions, taking into account land and water resources and the possibilities of raising yields by applications of inputs and technology. The results do not represent the possible or potential growth of production for the

TABLE 4

ANNUAL RATES OF GROWTH OF AGGREGATE DOMESTIC DEMAND (a)
1969-71 to 1978-80 AND (b) 1978-80 to 2000 (in %)

| Region | Meat | | Milk | | Cereals | | Oilseeds | |
|---|---|---|---|---|---|---|---|---|
| | (a) | (b) | (a) | (b) | (a) | (b) | (a) | (b) |
| N. Africa/Mid. East | 5.7 | 5.4 | 5.3 | 3.3 | 4.5 | 2.5 | 4.6 | 3.6 |
| Sub-Saharan Africa | 2.8 | 2.9 | 1.2 | 2.9 | 2.4 | 3.0 | 1.2 | 2.4 |
| EEC | 2.2 | 0.7 | 0.7 | 0.3 | 0.8 | 0.4 | 6.6 | 1.5 |
| Other Western Europe | 3.9 | 1.8 | 1.1 | 0.9 | 3.6 | 1.5 | 7.5 | 2.3 |
| USSR | 2.6 | 2.1 | 1.9 | 1.0 | 3.3 | 1.6 | 0 | 2.5 |
| Eastern Europe | 4.0 | 1.5 | 2.0 | 1.1 | 3.2 | 1.1 | 7.5 | 2.1 |
| S. Asia | 3.1 | 3.7 | 3.5 | 2.7 | 2.2 | 2.2 | 1.0 | 2.0 |
| E. Asia | 5.7 | 5.2 | 4.3 | 2.5 | 3.2 | 2.6 | 5.2 | 4.5 |
| Asian centrally planned economies | 4.4 | 3.1 | 4.4 | 3.0 | 3.8 | 1.7 | 2.0 | 2.9 |
| Oceania | 2.5 | 1.5 | -0.2 | 1.6 | 3.9 | 3.2 | 9.4 | 7.8 |
| Latin America | 3.7 | 3.8 | 3.2 | 3.1 | 3.6 | 2.7 | 4.2 | 3.5 |
| N. America | 2.1 | 0.9 | 0.7 | 0.9 | 0.4 | 1.2 | 4.0 | 1.3 |
| World | 3.1 | 2.4 | 1.7 | 1.5 | 2.6 | 1.8 | 3.8 | 2.3 |

Source: Fred Sanderson, "World Food Prospects to the Year 2000," *Food Policy* (November 1984), p. 366.

world. For the regions other than the EEC and North America, the growth in production of cereals are the projected changes. However, for the EEC the net exports of grain were apparently set at 20 million tons for 2000, not very far from the anticipated net exports for 1984-85.[2] The North American production growth is clearly demand limited—the region is considered to be the residual supplier of grain exports to the rest of the world and the production level for 2000 is set at the sum of domestic demand plus net exports. Consequently the annual growth rates of cereal production of 1.12 percent for the EEC and 1.35 for North America cannot be viewed as representing what is either technologically or economically possible, assuming real cereal prices similar to those of the late 1970's or early 1980's. For the world as a whole, there is a significant reduction in the projected annual growth of cereal production—from 2.6 percent actual growth in the 1970s to 1.83 percent projected for the rest of the century. For North America the difference between the actual growth in the 1970's and the projected growth for 1980-2000 is even greater than for the world—a decline from 3.5 percent to 1.35 percent. For the EEC the decline in growth rates is projected to be 50 percent. There are no technological or resource factors that would limit the growth rates for cereal output in North America or the EEC to the projected levels.

It is noted that for most regions of the world, except Sub-Saharan Africa, that most of the increased demand for food will come from increased production within the region (Sanderson 1984b, pp. 579-60). However, it is also probable that for most regions of the world that are now net importers of meat, cereals and oilseeds the absolute level of imports will increase. Thus there will be some increase in the dependence of the world for cereal imports upon North America and Oceania; for oilseeds there will be increased dependence upon the United States, Brazil and Argentina. But the growth of world trade for these products—and for meat as well—will be at a much slower annual rate for the rest of the century than for the 1970's.

The implications of these projections to U.S. farmers are striking and quite pessimistic. During the 1970's U.S. grain exports increased at an annual rate of 11 percent; for the rest of the century the projected growth rate is 2.2 percent. The growth of oilseed exports was 7 percent and is likely to fall to 2.4 percent. In the United States domestic demand is projected to grow even more slowly than export demand (Sanderson 1984b, p. 582). Consequently, if these projections are even close to the mark, U. S. farm output will be able to grow at a rate for the rest of the century that is half or less of the actual growth during the 1970's.

### Declining Prices of Food

The costs and prices of most crop products have declined for periods ranging from four to eight decades. This is after adjustment for the changes in the general price level. Table 5 presents data on the real export prices for the United States for wheat and corn from 1910 to date. Similar patterns can be found for most crop products (World Bank 1984). For example, Thai export prices of rice, deflated by the price index of manufactured products exported from the industrial countries to the developing countries, declined by 1.2 percent annually from 1950-52 to 198-82; soybean oil declined by 3.3 percent annually (approximately the same as other vegetable oils) and soybean meal declined by 1.8 percent each year. Real banana prices declined by 1.1 percent annually for the 30 year period.

The declining real prices of the major sources of calories reflect improvements in the productivity of resources engaged in agriculture. Even with the declining real prices, the farmers in most countries have shared in the economic growth that has occurred. In other words, as real per capita incomes have increased in most economies, the real incomes of farm families have also increased even though the prices of what they produced have been falling relative to all other prices. The only exceptions to the participation of farm people in the gains from economic growth have occurred where national policies are strongly biased against farm people, as has been true in many African countries. But where farmers have been treated with some degree of fairness, their real incomes and consumption have also increased. Such a result has been due to the growing productivity of their land, capital, labor and management.

TABLE 5

REAL EXPORT PRICES FOR WHEAT AND CORN, UNITED STATES, SELECTED YEARS, 1910-1913[a]

(1967 $ per ton)

| Calendar Year | Wheat | Corn | Calendar Year | Wheat | Corn |
|---|---|---|---|---|---|
| 1910-1914 | 100 | 74 | 1969 | 57 | 48 |
| 1925-1929 | 103 | 76 | 1970 | 53 | 52 |
| 1930-1934 | 79 | 85 | 1971 | 54 | 50 |
| 1935-1939 | 79 | 85 | 1972 | 54 | 46 |
| 1945-1949 | 122 | 94 | 1973 | 80 | 63 |
| 1950-1954 | 95 | 80 | 1974 | 110 | 79 |
| 1955-1959 | 69 | 61 | 1975 | 95 | 76 |
| 1960 | 65 | 53 | 1976 | 80 | 64 |
| 1961 | 69 | 52 | 1977 | 58 | 52 |
| 1962 | 70 | 52 | 1978 | 61 | 50 |
| 1963 | 69 | 56 | 1979 | 67 | 50 |
| 1964 | 69 | 57 | 1980 | 66 | 50 |
| 1965 | 62 | 57 | 1981 | 62 | 50 |
| 1966 | 62 | 56 | 1982 | 56 | 39 |
| 1967 | 64 | 54 | 1983 | 53 | 44 |
| 1968 | 60 | 48 | 1984 | 50 | 46 |

[a]The export prices are export unit values; the price deflator is the U.S. wholesale price index. Source: U.S. Department of Commerce, *Statistical Abstract of the United States*, various issues.

## Prospects for the Future

I have argued that there has been improvement in the nutritional status of poor people in the developing countries. This improvement has been made possible by significant improvements in productivity of resources used in producing food products, such as grains and vegetable oils, and by a major increase in the role of trade in providing access to world food supplies. In addition, for most of the developing countries there has been a rate of economic growth that has permitted increases in per capita income in spite of the increasing population.

The projections that I have presented point to continued improvement in the nutritional status in the developing countries. Based on these projections, I believe that it is clearly possible to substantially improve per capita food consumption in the developing countries, though realizing the potential improvement will require significant changes in national policies.There are, I am sure, some lingering doubts that make it difficult for many to accept what seems to be reasonably optimistic picture of the future. A number of arguments are presented when a more pessimistic view is put forward. I will now consider some of these points.

## Natural Resource Limitation

Most of the arguments used to support the conclusion that the growth of food output must slow down, or perhaps even eventually cease, are based upon natural resource limitations. These limitations are said to include: the amount of additional land which can be brought under cultivation is minimal; energy supplies are gradually being exhausted which will increase the cost of fertilizer and of pumping water used for irrigation; available soil is being lost due to diversion to other uses and to erosion; and the supply of fish can be expanded only at substantially higher cost and prices.

## Most Potential Land is Cultivated

The view that there remains very little land to bring under cultivation in the world and that this places a significant limitation on the expansion of food production is both factually incorrect and, even if true, largely irrelevant. There is a substantial potential for expanding the amount of cultivatable land in South America, Africa and Southeast Asia (World Food Conference). The amount of arable land in the developing market economies has increased during the 1970's, from 565 million hectares in 1970 to 598 million hectares in 1980 or by 5.8 percent (FAO 1980).

But the expansion of the cultivated area is probably not the lowest cost means of increasing food and agricultural production. The United States now has the same arable area that it did in 1950 though it is generally agreed that cropland in the United States could be increased by from 10 to 15 percent. However, farmers have not taken that approach in increasing crop production at an annual rate of about 2 percent over the past two decades. It has been cheaper to increase production by increasing yields per unit of land instead of increasing the arable area.

The developing countries, while continuing to expand the cultivated area, have also been successful in increasing yields. For 1961–65 to

1978-80 approximately two thirds of the 3 percent annual growth in cereal production can be attributed to higher yields (CYMMYT). For that period the growth of grain production in the developing countries was at the same or slightly higher rate than in the developed countries.

The emphasis upon the amount of cultivated land ignores the changes that can be made to improve the productive capacity of that land and to significantly increase the stability of production. One of the most important trends in the developing countries has been the increase in the amount of irrigation. In India the area of irrigated land has increased from 25.5 million hectares in 1961–65 to 39.1 million hectares in 1979. In China the increase was from 38.5 million to 49.2 million hectares for the same time period. These two countries have a large fraction of the irrigated land in the developing world, where the irrigated area increased from 70.0 million hectares in 1961–65 to 100.0 million hectares in 1979. India alone accounted for almost half of the increases for all developing countries (FAO 1980).

There has also been a significant though smaller increase in irrigated land in the industrial countries—from 27.2 million hectares in 1961–65 to 31.0 million hectares in 1979. Depending upon the particular situations, irrigated land yields from two to four times as much as the same land before it was irrigated. Thus irrigating one hectare of land is the same as "finding" one to three additional hectares of cropland even when the irrigated area had been cultivated before.

The RFF projections for 2000 assume that almost all of the increase in grain output will come from higher yields per hectare of planted area. Of the annual growth of production of 1.83 percent, only 0.27 percent is attributed to increased area. During the 1970's the area devoted to grain increased by 0.65 percent annually accounting for approximately a quarter of the increased output (Sanderson 1984a, p. 367).

**Adequacy of Land Resources**

Over the years a number of individuals and organizations have made estimates of the number of people that could be supported by the land resources of the world. Such estimates have varied enormously, depending upon the assumptions made about technology and the composition of the diet. Estimates of the "carrying capacity" of 40 billion and some even higher have been made. These large estimates compare to an estimated world population of about 6 billion in 2000. Such estimates need to be interpreted with care and their assumptions carefully understood.

The Food and Agriculture Organization (FAO) and the International Institute for Applied Systems Analysis (IIASA) have recently completed the most detailed study of the food production potentials of the developing world that has been made (Shah). Unfortunately the study does not include China due to the lack of comparable data. Estimates were made for soil–climate combinations for each area of approximately 10,000 hectares (less than 40 square miles). The production potentials of 15 of the most widely grown food crops and livestock production from grassland were assessed for each of the areas. The assessment was carried out for three different levels of technology: a low–level equivalent to presently practiced subsistence agriculture in some areas; a high–level equivalent to presently available high-yield farming technology, and an intermediate level representing a combination of the two levels.

The populations that could be supported in 2000 in the developing regions (excluding China and the remainder of East Asia) range from 3.0 billion at the low level of technology to 30.6 billion at the high level of technology. The more reasonable figure may be the intermediate level technology—a capacity of 12.4 billion. These population projections are only for the food that could be produced by rainfed agriculture. The potential population that could be supported from irrigated land, if fully developed, was projected at 2.6 billion. This projection implies an increase in irrigated area of about 50 percent and significant improvements to existing systems.

The supporting potentials for population in 2000 should be compared with the projected population for the countries included in the study. The population projected for 2000 is 3.6 billion. Thus the supportable population with low level technology, with the existing irrigated area, would be equal to the projected population for 2000.

I present these results to support the view that I have long held, namely that natural resources are not the limiting factor in determining food availability or consumption. Income levels are to a very large extent independent of the natural resource base of a country or region. What really counts is human capital and economic and political organization and the policies that are followed. In presenting the results of this study I do not want to imply, simply because land and natural resources are not the limiting factors in preventing adequate nutrition for every one, that it will be possible to make significant strides toward achieving the elimination of malnutrition in the world. Unfortunately that is not the case. Human institutions are often rather less tractable and malleable than nature. As I shall argue later, the fact that the potential for eliminating hunger and malnutrition exists does not mean that we can be complacent.

**Erosion**

In recent years there has been much attention given to the loss of soil resources, both in the United States and in the developing country. Lester

Brown of Worldwatch has perhaps given greatest emphasis to the issue. In addition, there are other ways that agricultural land may be lost (also emphasized by Brown), namely through transfer to nonagricultural uses such as roads, housing and airports. An important loss of farm land has occurred due to the construction of irrigation works based on water storage (Crosson).

Soil erosion does result in some loss of productive land. However, it seems easy to overestimate the probable effects. Few careful studies are available on the output effects of erosion that has occurred or is anticipated to occur in the years ahead. Crosson and Stout have made the most systematic study.

Erosion can be, and perhaps has been, more serious in some parts of the world than implied by the above discussion. This is particularly the case where ownership rights and the conditions of access to land are not well defined. The degradation of land under the commune system and other policies of the Mao regime in China have been well documented by Smil. The soil losses appear to have been enormous, but these losses were not due primarily to natural conditions. Rather, they reflect the failure to adequately define and enforce property rights in the land as well as the policy of forcing the expansion of grain production into unsuitable areas with fragile and erosive soils. Substantial changes on both scores have now occurred and it is quite likely that the amount of erosion has been substantially reduced.

Admittedly, in some parts of the world soil erosion is a serious problem requiring attention. Far too much of the recent and current discussion of erosion appears to be based on the assumption that farmers have neither the intelligence nor the knowledge required to conserve what is for them their most important resource—the land. Farmers are not lacking in intelligence nor do they behave in perverse ways unless misguided policies either force them to do so or make it in the interests of their families to do so. Price policies that depress farm prices and discriminate against agriculture reduce the incentives to conserve land. Institutional arrangements, such as common property with uncontrolled or poorly devised rules of access, can have adverse erosion consequences. No one should expect farmers to operate in other than their own interests and that of their families. Institutional arrangements should be devised that minimize the differences between private and social costs and returns. Until that occurs, it would be best for the rest of us to change the way rights to use property are allocated and to stop blaming farm people for the inevitable consequences of inappropriate legal and institutional arrangements.

## Other Limiting Factors

In addition to natural resource limitations, two other fears have been expressed that could have implications for consumers in developing countries. One is that rising incomes in industrial countries and the rapidly growing middle income countries will result in such rapid growth of demand for grain for feed as to limit the availability of grain to be used as food in the developing countries. The second is that agricultural products will be used as an energy source, presumably as the price of oil increases.

Neither of the two arguments is at all persuasive. The demand for grain for feed in the industrial countries has grown very slowly since the early 1970's; the only significant expansion has occurred in the USSR. It is true that the growth in the rapidly developing countries has continued at a high rate, but the base from which the growth occurs is so low that for the current century such added use of feed will remain relatively insignificant. In 1979–80 the feed use of grain in all of Asia (except for Japan), Africa and Latin America was only 56 million tons or 4 percent of world grain production. Since the late 1960's the annual growth rate of grain use as feed has been approximately 7 percent. If this rate of growth should be maintained until 2000, grain used as feed would increase to about 215 million tons or 9 percent of projected world production.

It is often said that modern agriculture is energy intensive and thus that food output would be adversely affected by increases in the price of energy. However, agricultural production is not particularly energy intensive in the United States or Western Europe. In the United States the energy used on farms is approximately 3 percent of the energy used in the country, and agriculture produces approximately 3 percent of the gross national product. If one takes the entire food chain, from the farm output sector through the marketing sector to delivery of food to the home, the same relationship holds true—the percentage of the nation's energy used and of the national gross product are approximately the same.

Two points are relevant. One is that U.S. farmers have reduced the amount of energy they have used relative to output in about the same proportion as all producers and consumers in the economy since the increase in real energy prices began in 1973. The second is we should not take a static view of the relationship between energy costs and the costs of farm inputs. This is well illustrated by fertilizer prices since 1970. Fertilizer, especially nitrogen fertilizer, is considered to be highly energy intensive. Yet improvements in the production of fertilizer over the past two decades have meant that the prices U.S. farmers have paid for fertilizer are now no higher relative to the prices of all farm inputs than was the case in 1967.[3]

### Research—A Strong Plus

One very important development that is ignored in many discussions of world food prospects and particularly the possibilities of increased production in the developing countries has been the rapid growth of expenditures on agricultural research over the past quarter century. Table 6 presents data on research expenditures as estimated by Robert Evenson. For the world and the developing regions there was an enormous growth in agricultural research expenditures during the 1960's. Growth slowed during the 1970's but even so, research expenditures in Latin America more than doubled and the much larger expenditures in Asia increased by almost 50 percent. For the two decades, the increase in research expenditures was lowest in Africa and highest in Asia. The 1980 expenditures in Africa were 3.6 times the 1959 level while the ratio was 5.8 for Latin America and 6.9 for Asia.

TABLE 6

AGRICULTURAL RESEARCH EXPENDITURES, 1959, 1970, AND 1980
AND SCIENTIFIC MANPOWER, 1980
(Million Constant 1980 US$)

|  | 1959 | 1970 | 1980 | Manpower (Man-years) 1980 |
|---|---|---|---|---|
| Western Europe | 275 | 919 | 1,490 | 19,540 |
| North America and Oceania | 760 | 1,485 | 1,722 | 13,607 |
| Eastern Europe and USSR | 568 | 1,282 | 1,493 | 51,614 |
| Latin America | 80 | 216 | 462 | 8,534 |
| Africa | 119 | 252 | 425 | 8,088 |
| Asia | 261 | 1,205 | 1,798 | 46,656 |
| World Total | 2,063 | 5,359 | 7,390 | 148,039 |

Source: Robert E. Evenson, "The IARC's: Evidence of Impact on National Research and Extension Programs," Yale Economic Growth Center, unpublished paper, 1985, p. 1a.

It is worth noting that there is a time lag of 7 to 10 years between research expenditures and the increases in productivity at the farm level. Consequently we have yet to see much of the effect of the substantially higher research expenditures that occurred from 1975 to date. This is a very positive sign.

Increasing agricultural output is primarily a function of science and technology, on the one hand, and the availability of modern inputs, on the other hand. We have seen evidence of a substantial growth in research expenditures. We can also trace the spread of modern inputs in the developing countries, especially those in Asia and Latin America. The modern inputs that I refer to are primarily biological and chemical, not mechanical. In particular, the modern inputs that help produce higher yields per unit of land are improved seeds, including hybrid seeds, fertilizer, insecticides, herbicides and disease controlling materials. While machinery can have some positive effects on yields, primarily by permitting more timely operations and making possible double and triple cropping, machinery serves primarily to replace labor and not land.

In my opinion, the grain yield data in Table 7 tell several remarkable stories. Modern agriculture is of recent origin in the world. Even in 1934–38, hybrid seeds had not yet influenced crop yields, nor was any significant amount of chemical fertilizer being used on grain crops, certainly not in the developing countries.

TABLE 7

AVERAGE GRAIN YIELDS OF DEVELOPING AND INDUSTRIALIZED
COUNTRIES DURING SELECTED PERIODS, 1934-1984
(Metric tons per Hectare)

|  | 1934-38 | 1952-56 | 1969-70 | 1982-84 |
|---|---|---|---|---|
| Developing Countries | 1.15 | 1.15 | 1.41 | 2.08 |
| Industrialized Countries | 1.15 | 1.37 | 2.14 | 2.73 |

Source: FAO, Production Yearbooks, various issues.

The first story is that in the late 1930's, the grain yields in the developing and industrial countries were the same. Thus prior to the introduction of high yielding varieties and the use of any significant amount of chemical fertilizers on grains, the yields were primarily determined by the natural conditions—soils and climates. And the yield outcomes were the same.

The second story is that grain yields in the industrial countries increased significantly between 1934–38 and 1952–56, while yields in the developing countries remained unchanged. Over the next 15 years grain yields in the industrial countries increased by 56 percent compared to just 23 percent in the developing countries. The new high yielding varieties and significant use of fertilizer on grains was in its infancy by 1969. But by the early 1980's, part of the yield gap was closed by an increase in yields in the developing countries of 48 percent compared to only a 28 percent increase in the industrial countries.

The third story is that the developing countries can obviously take advantage of the important and relevant features of modern agriculture to increase their grain production. To some considerable degree, the significant expansion of research referred to earlier is now paying off. Thus, future gains can be anticipated with a higher level of certainty.

### Incentives, Policies and Infrastructure

Farmers, like the rest of us, respond to incentives. In far too many countries the incentive structure is seriously distorted and to the disadvantage of farm people. In all too many countries few fates can be worse than that of farmers who are efficient producers, and thus have been exporters of traditional crops. Nothing apparently attracts the avarice of a finance minister or other high public official more than a product that is exported across national borders and is perhaps forced to use a single port.

Let me illustrate this point with a limited number of examples. The time period is a recent one, 1976–80. During those years, if you were a producer of cocoa and lived in Cameroon, Ghana, Ivory Coast or Togo, your government graciously permitted you to retain from 25 to 45 percent of the export value of your cocoa. In other words, the government taxed or otherwise took away from you 55 to 75 percent of the export value of the cocoa. If you were a producer of groundnuts or peanuts and lived in Malawi, Mali, Senegal, Sudan or Zambia, you were allowed to keep from 43 to 71 percent of the export value of your crop. And if you were a producer of coffee in Togo, the government took 77 percent of the export value leaving you with just 23 percent (World Bank 1981a).

Egypt has followed a policy of low farm prices and even lower consumer prices for important food products. In 1980, the rice producer received less than 30 percent of the international market price, the wheat producer less than 70 percent, the sugar producer less than 50 percent. Consumer prices were even lower compared to international prices, with the rice price at less than 20 percent and wheat at less than 40 percent (Schuh 1983). Thus it should come as no surprise that Egypt is no longer a net exporter of agricultural products and imports a large percentage of its basic food supply.

Many developing countries also exploit their agricultures by maintaining an overvalued exchange rate. Such exchange rates act as a tax upon exports, including agricultural exports which often account for the majority of foreign exchange earnings. When the currency is overvalued, this means that when the export earnings in foreign currency are translated into the domestic currency, the exporter receives less domestic currency than would have been true if the exchange rate were at its true level. But it is not only agricultural exports that are taxed in this way. An overvalued currency also makes it relatively cheap to import farm products if you have access to foreign exchange (dollars, marks, yen, for example) at the official exchange rate. Thus if the currency is overvalued by 25 percent—a not unusual overvaluation and much less than some—this means that if food is imported in sufficient quantity it will drive down the price to local producers by the amount of overvaluation.

The current African food situation has resulted from upwards of two decades of neglect of agriculture and rural areas. In an important article published in *Science* in early 1981, Uma Lele began her article by noting that in less than a decade "Africa is facing a second severe food crisis." She noted that the poor crop "can yet again be explained as a result of drought." Then she adds: "But the continent's growing vulnerability to crop failures is by no means unexpected. In most African countries it appears to be part of a long-term trend." (p.547).

She emphasizes a number of factors that are responsible for the long-term trend toward increased food vulnerability. They include a slow rate of growth of national income, rapid population growth, and a policy of neglect of agriculture. One evidence of the neglect of rural areas and over-emphasis on urban areas is the much larger rural–urban income disparities that prevail in Africa as opposed to many Asian countries. She notes that in Africa the rural–urban income ratios typically range between 1:4 and 1:9 compared with Asiatic countries with ratios of 1:2 and 1:2.5 (p.547).

After noting that most of the planned development expenditures were allocated to sectors other than agriculture, she notes that most of the tax revenue has come from agriculture: "Peasant agriculture is highly taxed by fixing low prices for its products. . . Agricultural taxation helps keep urban food prices low and finances modernization through the many capital–intensive investments such as construction of new capital cities, stadiums, manufacturing and processing plants, and airports" (p. 549).

Robert H. Bates, a political scientist, has undertaken an exhaustive study of the basis for the agricultural policies that have been followed in Africa. His starting point was the acceptance of the conclusion that farm people are intelligent and rational. He believes that there is a rational basis for the types of agricultural policies being followed in Africa, though as he argues in this quotation some of the long run effects may not have been fully recognized. Let me quote:

> The agricultural policies of the nations of Africa confer benefits on highly concentrated and organized groupings. They spread costs over the masses of the unorganized. They have helped to evoke the self-interested assent of powerful interests to the formation of a new political order, and have provoked little organized resistance. In this way, they have helped to generate a political equilibrium. But in the longer run, the costs inflicted by these

policies are being passed on to members of the policy-making coalition, and the configurations that were once in equilibrium are now becoming politically unstable.

Among those excluded from the immediate rewards of the new political order are the mass of farmers. For the benefit of others, they are subjected to policies that violate their interests. But the effects of these policies are increasingly harmful to everyone. Reducing the incentives to grow food leads to reduced food production; the result is higher food prices and waves of discontent in the urban centers. The coups and countercoups that have recently swept West Africa owe their origin, as we have noted, in part to discontent over higher food prices. And they show how policies that have been designed to serve the interests of powerful groups impose costs which in the long run affect everyone, thereby undercutting the positions of advantage they have helped to create and disrupting the political order.

Reducing the incentives to produce export crops is also proving politically costly. The result of adverse incentives has in some cases been a measurable decline in the production of exports, with a resultant loss of public revenues and foreign exchange (Bates 1981, p. 129).

It is difficult to add to what Bates has written. He puts the policies in a political and social context broader than I have used. But his basic conclusion is essentially the same—the agricultural policies followed by most African countries have resulted in a lower level of food output than it was reasonable to expect, given the resources available. But he makes the additional point that the consequences of these policies have threatened and continue to threaten the social and political stability of many African states.

## Poverty is the Primary Cause of Hunger and Malnutrition

If people are hungry or malnourished, for the vast majority of such persons the cause is not a lack of available food but poverty. So the primary avenue by which malnutrition can be reduced and eventually largely eliminated is through increasing the incomes of poor people. Only in limited areas of the world, such as in parts of Sub-Saharan Africa, can it now be said that the lack of readily available food is an important cause of hunger. There remain some parts of the world that are isolated in the same way large parts of India and China were a century ago. A local crop failure could, then for a large percentage of the world's population, and today for a small percentage, result in famine because food could not be brought to the stricken area in time. Sen, in his book *Poverty and Famines,* has shown quite strikingly that in four famines of the last half century it was loss of income for certain population groups that was the cause of famine, not the unavailability of food.

There is, however, an interrelationship between agricultural productivity and malnutrition that should not be neglected. The majority of the world's poor people (the World Bank has estimated 80 percent) reside in rural areas. Thus increasing the productivity of agricultural areas, especially the productivity of people, through research, education, infrastructure investment in roads and other forms of communication, will increase rural incomes and thus make such people less vulnerable to malnutrition. Making agriculture more productive not only adds to the food supply but equally important increases income and in both ways contributes to reduction of malnutrition.

The particular focus of the previous two paragraphs is sometimes put rather differently. The different focus is that the primary cause of hunger in the world is distribution—there are adequate supplies of food in the world and if these supplies were distributed more equitably hunger and malnutrition could be eliminated. My focus is that we must be concerned about both distribution *and* production and that these two are interrelated in the lower income rural areas of the world. They are also interrelated in urban areas since we have seen that the increase in agricultural productivity has resulted in steady and significant declines in the real prices of cereals, the major source of calories for low income people.

It is well and good to consider changes in the distribution of food among nations, and among peoples within nations, as the primary answer to hunger and malnutrition. But we must consider the important implications of efforts that involve transfers among nations. Obviously, it is not desirable to create long run dependence of any country or group of people upon others who live faraway. More importantly, the efforts and resources that would be required to modify the distribution of food by direct transfers might well have greater effect if used to increase the productivity of low income families. This is almost certainly likely for the rural poor. For urban poor the distributive measures may well be effective in reducing malnutrition and hunger, though the governmental costs of such measures may over time severely limit what can be done or, as in the case of Sri Lanka, require most of the effort to be abandoned.

**Man Not Nature is the Barrier**

A major conclusion of my analysis of the prospective world food supply situation is that improvements in per capita food supplies depend to a much greater extent upon the actions of man than upon any restraints imposed by nature. By actions of man, I mean the policies that governments follow—whether those policies encourage or discourage farm people in their use of resources, or provide or do not provide farmers with the means to improve their productivity.

This conclusion seems so self evident from even rather casual observation of the performance of agriculture and of available food supplies in different countries, that it is hard to understand why there continues to be an emphasis upon natural resource limitations. The sad state of the food situation in Africa is not the result of a lack of natural resources. In fact, it is generally conceded that Africa is much better endowed with natural resources per capita than Asia and as well endowed as Latin America. Yet per capita food production has increased rather steadily in Asia and Latin America while declining in much of Africa since 1970.

However, the strongest example of the effects of policies upon agricultural performance is now available for anyone who wishes to look. I refer to the amazing turnaround in agricultural productivity and output growth in China since 1978. Since 1979 there has been a reversal in Chinese agricultural policy; the changes are as revolutionary as the land reform of the 1950's or the creation of the communes in the late 1950's. The stifling restraints upon individual effort and initiative that were an integral aspect of the commune system, especially from 1965 to 1977, have been abolished. In most villages the land has been assigned to individual households, first for three years and now for periods ranging from 10 to 15 years. Starting with 1985, required or quota deliveries of most farm products to the state were abolished and the state purchasing agency enters into contracts with farm families.

The total output of the villages which were the former communes, increased at an annual rate of 8.5 percent from 1978 to 1984. The output of the villages is defined by the Chinese as gross agricultural output. However, this measure of output includes nonfarm products-industrial, handicrafts, and the processing of agricultural products. Due to the significant release of labor from strictly agricultural pursuits, the output of the nonfarm sidelines increased more rapidly than did agricultural output. The annual increase for the sidelines was about 14 percent while the annual growth of agricultural output, as more traditionally defined, increased at about 7.3 percent, or a little more than 50 percent in six years. Such a high growth rate for agricultural products is very unusual, especially for a period as long as six years.

While it is possible that some part of the growth of farm production has been associated with favorable weather, though I do not say that has been the case, the output record is still quite remarkable. It is even more remarkable that it was achieved with only very modest growth in the volume of inputs used. In fact, if we had an accurate measure of the labor input, it is quite possible that total inputs used in Chinese agriculture declined between 1978 and 1984. But accepting the employment data, the volume of inputs—land, labor, machinery and current purchased inputs — increased by 25 percent.

In addition to the organizational and institutional changes that greatly increased the freedom of the individual and family to choose how they used their resources, in 1979 the prices that the state paid for most farm products were increased by approximately 25 percent and a bonus that was 30 to 50 percent greater than the base price was paid for deliveries in excess of the quotas. The net effect of the price changes was to increase the average price received for deliveries to the state by more than a third.

Other changes were to remove restrictions upon private sideline activities. During the Cultural Revolution many villages prevented farm families from producing vegetables on the land in their house area. The production of handicrafts was frowned upon and in some cases prohibited. Most of the local markets, some of which had operated for hundreds of years, were closed down. Buying and selling even at the local level was considered to be capitalistic, and farm people were prevented from making private sales to urban consumers. These types of restrictions were lifted after 1976 and 1977, some quite rapidly and others much more gradually. By 1981 most such restraints imposed from governmental units or by commune officials had been eliminated. The response in terms of increased activity and energy was substantial, indeed.

These changes were in addition to the incentives resulting from the various forms of the responsibility system that started to emerge in 1979 and 1980. Under the responsibility systems, a connection between one's productivity and one's reward was established, where such a connection had hardly existed for as long as 15 years. In the most radical era, a significant fraction of the net income of production teams was distributed on an equal per capita basis; only part of the income was associated with work effort and the association with the productive outcome of the work effort was tenuous indeed.

The point that I wish to make, without belaboring it further, is that the Chinese experience since 1978 indicates how much releasing the energies and intelligence of farm people can accomplish with minimal increases in inputs or resources when you start from a situation in which governmental intervention has had a repressive effect upon incentives and production. And such effects exist in far too many countries. Whatever else one wishes to learn from the Chinese experiments, it is clear that farm people do know how to manage their resources in an effective manner when given a chance. This is true even though the size of the agricultural area commanded by each family is exceedingly small. China has approximately 185 million households and about 100 million hectares (245 million acres) of cropland. Thus each household has less than 1.5 acres of cropland, on the average.

It was only a few years ago that China suffered from famines, including one in 1981 for which it requested international assistance (Johnson 1981, p. 209). And it was less than a quarter century ago that it had the world's most horrible famine, as measured by the number of people who died. By its policy changes alone, China has greatly diminished the possibility of a major famine occurring again. The per capita output of grain in China in 1976–78 was the same as two decades earlier, 1956–58. In just six years per capita grain output has increased by more than a fourth. The substantial output growth must have been an important factor in the decision to abolish required deliveries of grain and most other farm products. A few years ago it was thought essential to pay a substantial premium to induce more deliveries to meet the needs of cities and industries. Now the Chinese government is embarrassed by greater deliveries than it can handle. While this is certainly a temporary situation, it is one that few anticipated would occur.

### Conclusion

The world possesses the resources, both natural and human, to achieve a significant improvement in the nutrition of the people of the low income countries by the end of this century. Thus, by the end of this century famine and hunger due to local production shortfalls could be eliminated for all but a tiny percentage of the world's population. Further, the amount of food consumed can be increased to levels that provide adequate nutrition for almost all.

But these desirable improvements will not occur unless efforts are made to make them occur. Farm people in all countries must be treated fairly and equitably and permitted to share in economic growth. The governmental interventions that now do so much harm—low farm prices and trade restrictions—must be modified if not removed. Finally, farmers must be assured of an adequate and stable supply of modern farm inputs at reasonable prices.

If farm people are given a reasonable chance, they will surely respond; and they will respond in such a way as to benefit all of mankind.

D. Gale Johnson, noted agricultural economist, is the Eliakim Hastings Moore Distinguished Service Professor at the University of Chicago. Dr. Johnson received the Ph.D from Iowa State College. He has served as a consultant and economic advisor to many government agencies concerned with the economics of food production and distribution. Currently, he is serving as editor of the *Journal of Economic Development and Cultural Change*. Among his many publications are: "The Politics Food: Producing and Distributing the World's Food Supply," "Food and Agricultural Policy for the 1980's" and "The Role of Markets in the World Food Economy".

# FOOTNOTES

[1]This section of the paper draws heavily on Johnson (1985).

[2]U.S. Department of Agriculture, Economic Research Service, *Western Europe: Outlook and Situation Report,* RS-85-6, May 1985, pp. 10-11. Grain exports were 24.1 million tons and grain imports were 5.8 million tons for net exports of 18.3 million tons.

[3]Based on prices paid by farmers in April 1985, the price index for all production items was 283 with 1970=100. For fertilizer the price index was 285. Thus fertilizer prices did not increase more than all prices paid for items used in production. Source: U.S. Department of Agriculture.

# REFERENCES

Antle, John M. 1984. Human capital, infrastructure, and the productivity of Indiana rice farmers. *Journal of Development Economics* 14: 163–81.

Bale, Malcolm D. and Duncan, Ronald C. n.d. Food prospects in the developing countries.

Barney, Gerald O., Study Director. 1982. *The global 2000 report to the President.* New York: Penguin.

Bates, Robert H. 1981. *Markets and states in tropical Africa: The political basis of agricultural policies.* Berkeley: University of California Press.

China State Statistical Bureau. 1983. *Statistical yearbook.*

Crosson, Pierre R., ed. 1982. *The cropland crisis: Myth or reality?* Washington, D.C.: Resources for the Future.

Crosson, Pierre and A.T. Stout. 1983. *Productivity effects of cropland erosion in the United States.* Washington, D.C.: Resources for the Future.

Evenson, Robert E. 1985. The IARC's: Evidence of impact on national research and extension programs. Unpublished paper, Yale Economic Growth Center, 1a.

Food and Agricultural Organization of the United Nations (FAO). *Agriculture: Toward 2000.* Rome: FAO.

1980. *FAO Production Yearbook.* Rome: FAO. 1980

Fogel, Robert W. n.d.

International Maize and Wheat Improvement Center (CIMMYT). 1981. *World wheat facts and figures. Report one.* Mexico F.D.: CIMMYT.

Johnson, D. Gale. 1981. Food and agriculture of the centrally planned economies: Implications for the world food system. *Essays in Contemporary Economic Problems: Demand, Productivity, and Population.* ed. Wm. Fellner, 171–213. Washington, D.C.: The American Enterprise Institute.

———1985. A World food system: Actuality or promise? Perspectives in Biology and Medicine.

Johnson, D. Gale and Schuh, G. Edward, eds. 1983. *The role of markets in the world food economy.* Boulder: Westview Press.

Lele, Uma. 1981. Rural Africa: Modernization, equity, and long-term development. *Science* 211 (6 February 1981): 547–553.

Mollett, J. A. 1985. The key role of food imports in dietary improvements in developing countries—and their cost. *Outlook on Agriculture* 14(1): 27–34.

Sanderson, Fred H. 1984. World food prospects to the year 2000. *Food Policy* (November): 363–74

———1984. An assessment of global demand for U.S. agricultural products to the year 2000: Economic and policy dimensions. *American Journal of Agricultural Economics* 66 (5). (December 1984): 577–84.

Schuh, G. Edward. 1983. The world food situation. *American Journal of Agricultural Economics.* (May).

Sen, Amartya. 1981. *Poverty and famines; An essay on entitlement and deprivation.* Oxford: Clarendon Press.

Shah, M.M., *et al.* 1985. *People, land and food production—Potentials in the developing world.* Collaborative Paper. Laxenburg, Austria: International Institute for Applied Systems Analysis, CP–85–11.

Swanson, Earl R. and Earl O. Heady. 1984. Soil erosion in the United States. In *The Resourceful Earth,* eds. Julian Simon and Herman Kahn, 202–223. New York: Basil Blackwell.

U. S. Department of Agriculture, Economic Research Service. 1985. *Western Europe: Outlook and Situation Report,* RS–85–6 (May), 10–11.

World Bank. 1981. *Accelerated development in sub-Saharan Africa.* Washington, D.C.: World Bank.

---1980-1985. *World Development Report.* Washington, D.C.: World Bank, annual publication, various issues.

World Food Conference. 1974. Assessment of the world food situation, Present and future and the world food problems, Proposals for national and international action. In *Selected Materials for the Use of the U. S. Congressional Delegation to the World Food Conference.* Subcommittee on Foreign Agricultural Policy of the Committee on Agriculture and Forestry, United States Senate, 93d Congress, 2d Session, October 30, 1974. Washington: U.S. Government Printing Office.

# LIFEBOAT ETHICS: A RADICAL APPROACH

## Garrett Hardin

"Surely a civilization that is clever enough to put a man on the moon should be able to solve the problem of——!" How often we have heard such a sentence since July 1969, when the first men landed on the moon! The form of the sentence is constant; only the words in the blank space change. Hunger? Poverty? Inadequate housing? War? Injustice? The sentence serves all causes.

Whatever posterity may say of our generation, it won't fault us for lack of ambition to solve great social problems. Even the word "problem" reveals our ambition. Until about two centuries ago no one called hunger, poverty or injustice a problem. Instead the names for these misfortunes were regarded as merely definitions of the world as it is.

Now we see every unpleasant thing as a problem, and presume (without thinking much about the matter) that every problem has a solution. We conveniently forget that some problems don't have solutions. Take, for instance, the problem of constructing a perpetual motion machine. No matter how much we may want to find a solution to that problem, no matter how hard some people may try, scientists are convinced that a solution will never be found. Arguments brought forward more than a century ago by Maxwell and Boltzmann seem so simple, so irrefutable, that sane men no longer look for the will-o'-the wisp of self–generating energy. (The energy of the system must be self–generating to compensate for inevitable frictional losses. Friction, in the broadest sense, is another problem we will never solve. The apparent asymptote for frictional losses is lowered from time to time, but it is always something greater than zero.)

What about hunger and poverty? Should these be regarded as problems that have solutions, or are they merely inescapable aspects of the human condition? The social sciences have yet to produce their Maxwells and Boltzmanns, so there is some excuse for assuming that these misfortunes are problems, which justifies our looking for solutions.

A defiant approach to hunger was made in November of 1974 by Henry Kissinger, who was then Secretary of State. Speaking to the United Nations World Food Conference, he said: "Today we must proclaim a bold objective—that within a decade no child will go to bed hungry, that no family will fear for its next day's bread, and that no human being's future and capacities will be stunted by malnutrition." Brave words, these: but eleven years have passed since this stirring call was issued in Rome, and the number of hungry and malnourished children is greater than ever. Why have we so undeniably failed?

It was not for want of trying. Rich countries channeled billions of dollars to the poor; we *tried*. It won't do to offer the excuse of bad weather, because weather always varies between good and bad. In the perspective of world history the past decade has not been exceptional. National planning must allow for cyclical climate.

What about political injustice? This is often a contributing factor, but it would not be so important if every country had plenty of food. Whenever and wherever there is scarcity, the struggle for existence creates political turmoil.The powerful oppress the powerless. Political radicals and tender-hearted reformers like to point to political injustice as a cause of human suffering. So it sometimes is, but injustice can also be a *consequence* of the anticipation of suffering that comes with desperate competition under conditions of overpopulation. Injustice and want are elements in a circular system of causation. (Should not the U.S. take this into account in shaping its national policies toward Latin America?)

We solved the problem of putting a man on the moon in less than a decade after President Kennedy persuaded Congress in 1961 that it was a problem with a solution. But by now it should be clear that our progress towards solving "the hunger problem" has been, if anything, negative: we get farther from the solution all the time. We should begin to suspect that the elimination of hunger is significantly different from landing on the moon; and that our successes in space are irrelevant to the human problems at home. We must look for other approaches to the perdurable problem of poverty and of hunger which is one manifestation of poverty.

Let us start out on the road to a proper understanding of the hunger problem with a meditation on an oft-quoted statement by Albert Einstein: *Raffiniert ist der Herr Gott, aber Boschaft ist Er nicht —*" Subtle is the Lord, but he is not malicious." Guided by this deep faith, Einstein made astounding discoveries in the physical sciences. Such an attitude is universally fruitful in the physical sciences; but as soon as we put living organisms, particularly the human species, into the picture the game changes. Something like *Bosheit*—malice—enters in. Malice may not be the best word. Other possibilities are malevolence, resentment, obduracy, treachery, reactivity, and egocentricity. As far as I know, the English language has no suitable word for the ingrained responses that thwart solutions to certain sorts of problems. Perhaps no language does. The difficulty can best be exposed through an ostensive approach, a finger pointing approach.

I am going to do this in a way that may shock the reader. We are so used to looking for "breakthroughs" at the "leading edge of science" that we shamefully neglect the wisdom encapsulated in ancient writings. We think that the problem of hunger will be solved by developing superior strains of plants, or bigger catchment basins for dams, or more extensive irrigation systems, or more economical ways to use water, or hydroponics, or harvesting the seas, or some other proposed solution. An immense faith in gadgetry causes us to overlook the fact that the great technological accomplishments of the past have brought about no enduring progress in diminishing hunger. Doing more of the same will be just a spinning of the wheels. We need to pay attention to a paramount principle clearly stated more than two thousand years ago. I refer to the words of Koheleth, the Preacher, in *Ecclesiastes 5:11:* "When goods are increased, they are increased that eat them."

This wisdom, which we may call *Koheleth's Principle,* makes a mockery of all attempts to get rid of hunger by any technology that merely increases the supply of food. Biological forces, unless curbed, increase the demand without limit. In a limited world, and no other is available to us, only by controlling demand can we hope to do away with hunger and want.

To a species that is used to getting its way, and modern man spoiled by the marvels of technology is certainly such an animal, Koheleth seems to be describing a malicious state of affairs. To put it in the context of our space program, it is as though the moon, on noting the approach of Apollo-Saturn 11, should have revved up its lunar motors and retreated into outer space, thus preventing the three astronauts from ever landing on its surface. Such lunar behavior would have deserved the name of *Bosheit,* treachery or malicious reactivity. Fortunately, the purely physical world does not thwart us thus.

But the biological world does so thwart us. Living organisms *react* to the physical world and to each other. Feed a population that suffers from hunger, and you not only diminish the hunger temporarily, but you also increase hunger in the long run as today's population responds to increased food supplies by producing a larger population to make greater demands on the resources tomorrow. That is the deep truth recorded in *Ecclesiastes.*

Two thousand years later Koheleth's Principle still holds, and Darwinian biology tells us why. Consider what happens during a period when resources are in excess. Most members of a species will convert these resources into new offspring; but you can postulate, if you wish, that some individuals will not. The result is the offspring of those that obey Koheleth's Principle will increase relative to the offspring of the postulated group that does not. Darwinism is implicit in Koheleth's Principle; in fact, without the Darwinian foundation the Biblical passage is merely an *obiter dictum,* an unsupported statement made in passing. With Darwinism, Koheleth's Principle becomes a necessary truth.

In a competitive world the payoff goes to those who use the resources at hand to create a demand for more resources. No technological invention can countermand this Biblical-Darwinian truth. The inventions that can set it to one side lie in the realm of politics and social arrangements. In the long run, the so-called shortages of supply can be solved only by controlling "longages" of demand. "Demand" is a psychological concept, an entity internal to living organisms and hence beyond the purview of the physical sciences. *Der Herr Gott* has given us no assurances about the behavior of demand. This is *our* problem.

Are you shocked by Koheleth's Principle? If so, yours is a modern shock: most men and women, over most of human history, if they thought about population at all, agreed with Koheleth (and with the Darwin who was yet to be born; and also with Malthus). Listen to Tertullian in the third century A.D.: "As our demands grow greater, our complaints against nature's inadequacy are heard by all. The scourges of pestilence, famine, wars and earthquakes have come to be regarded as a blessing to overcrowded nations, since they serve to prune away the luxuriant growth of the human race." Tertullian was one of the "fathers" of the Christian religion. In his time, and for a millenium and a half afterward, most Christians agreed with Tertullian that pestilence, famine, wars and earthquakes were best seen as blessings, of a sort. Why, then, have religious attitudes changed recently?

Statistically speaking, there has been a decline in Bible-oriented religion in the past two centuries. Many people today don't look to the Bible for guidance; and many who loudly profess to revere it, read it only selectively. It appears that the wisdom of the book of *Ecclesiastes* is seldom drawn upon by today's Bible-worshippers.

What is the predominant religion of our time, in our part of the world? I think the "Man from Mars," trying to deduce the religion of Earthlings from their actions, would identify the idea of Progress as our most powerful religion. Our faith in technology is almost unlimited; unthinkingly we assume that every human problem can be converted into a technical problem, which can then be solved by purely technological means. "Look," say the worshippers of technological Progress, "pestilence used to be regarded as a visitation of God. Now we know that germs are the cause, and we have licked them by technological means."

Well, that takes care of one of Tertullian's four "blessings": but what about the other three—earthquakes, wars and famines? The progress we've made dealing with earthquakes is largely prudential, i.e., the enacting of adequate building codes. As for wars, the only progress we've made there (and that, very recently) is the final realization that no full-scale war can be won from here on out. (But it may take another generation, if we survive the interval, before we are governed by people who understand this.) As for famines, because of the reactive effect of Koheleth's Principle, all our technological progress has served only to move the number of those who suffer to a higher level.

The denial of Koheleth's Principle by the religion of Progress has been strengthened by another thread of thought, which also has its origin in religion. At issue is the question of the distribution of the earth's goods among the human inhabitants thereof. No healthy-minded person likes to be a witness to human suffering. Since the second World War, progress in the transmission of information has outpaced all other forms of progress. For the cost of mere pennies we can now observe the starvation of multitudes half a world away. Empathy, a biological attribute of most vertebrate species, including our own, leads us to want to do something about known suffering, whether near or distant. We try to follow a simple directive of the Christian fathers that was, ironically, adopted by Karl Marx who hated religion.

In the Acts of the Apostles, Luke describes an early Christian commune to which members gave all that they had. Thereafter, from the common store, "distribution was made unto every man according as he had need." This verse found its echo in 1875 in Marx's "Critique of the Gotha Program." In his blueprint for the ideal society, Marx laid down the rule of distribution in these now famous words: "From each according to his ability, to each according to his needs." Empathy makes us want to follow the Christian-Marxist rule; but Intellect cautions us to Think.

The Marxist formula perfectly epitomizes the nature of a common pool of resources from which each member can take according to his needs *as he perceives them.* The ultimate outcome is tragic, as I have argued at length in my essay, "The Tragedy of the Commons." After nearly twenty years of being examined by specialists in many fields, it is fair to say that the thesis of this essay is now part of the accepted wisdom of science. It fits in perfectly with the insight of Koheleth; but it is not compatible with the advice given by Luke and Marx. The ultimate collapse of tens of thousands of communes over the centuries, as well as the malfunctioning of many other Christian-Marxist arrangements, constitute overwhelming empirical evidence that making need the primary criterion for distribution simply won't work.

Why, in the face of all this evidence, do we repeatedly resurrect the Christian-Marxist scheme of distribution? I think the answer lies in our failure to appreciate the importance of *scale effects.* "From each according to his ability, to each according to his needs" is a pretty good description of the way a successful family should operate. It applies to a nuclear family, it may even apply to an extended family. But when it is made the rule in larger groups, disaster sooner or later overtakes the participants.

The most convincing evidence we have of this is the experience of the Hutterite communities in the northwest of the United States and adjacent Canadian provinces. The religious commitment and the rural simplicity of

Hutterite life create the most favorable environment for the operation of the Christian–Marxist distribution scheme; but these earnest people have found that it simply won't work once the size of the group has passed the century mark. As an engineer would put it, the Christian–Marxist scheme "does not scale up" beyond 100. Beyond that approximate number, the social value of an individual's performance, not his need, must be made the primary criterion for the distribution of income and resources. It is interesting to note that a spokesman for post-Mao China has explicitly acknowledged this necessity.

Unfortunately, common language shows little recognition of scale effects. Marshall McLuhan's "global village" is a monstrous marriage of incompatibles: the peculiar virtues (and defects) of a village of a hundred people simply do not scale up to a globe of nearly five billion. The warm and seductive term "the family of man" is another monstrosity. There is no way that the amount of trust that can be enjoyed by a really good nuclear family can be extended to the whole human species. The 19th-century political activist, Pierre–Joseph Proudhon, saw this clearly when he said: "If all the world is my brother, then I have no brother." Without *otherhood,* the precious qualities of brotherhood are lost, and people need brotherhood to stay healthy.

The term "Spaceship Earth" also deserves criticism. In popular rhetoric it implies a commitment to the creation of a worldwide commons, with distribution to each person (or each nation) according to need. If we follow this advice we will soon find that the sharing of wealth that we intended has metamorphosed into a sharing of poverty.

In the long run the commonizing of wealth and income leads to tragedy. Among nations, as among peoples, irresponsible systems of *sharing* on the basis of need must be replaced by responsible systems of *exchange* on the basis of productivity. This is why I have urged that we avoid the term "Spaceship Earth" with its implication of the commonization of resources and the abandonment of group responsibility. Far more appropriate is the term "Lifeboat Ethics", which implies the existence of many separate operational units, each of which is responsible for tailoring its demands to fit its resources. A still better term would be "Island Ethics", which also emphasizes local responsibility. I have called this "a radical approach" because, sadly, responsibility is a radical idea in our time. In the long run, meaningful responsibility minimizes suffering.

But compassion cries out for us to consider the short run. Can't we do something for those who are in desperate need now, while we also strive for long-run benefits?

A concrete example should help at this point. Let's take Ethiopia, which is on everyone's mind these days. Ethiopia has 36 million people, many of whom are now starving. In recent years the growth rate of her population has been 2.1 percent per year. If external aid succeeds in reducing starvation from the present high level to the "normal" level for this unfortunate country, by my calculations there will be 756,000 more Ethiopians next year who need to be fed. If external aid repeats its miracle again the following year, the number of Ethiopians in need will be increased even more—by 772,000. And the year after that the increase will rise to 788,000. Population increase is like compound interest in a bank account. In the light of this reality, Koheleth's Principle becomes more frightening.

Compassion is common, but understanding is rare. Compassion is praised, but understanding is denigrated. Giving to Ethiopia is fashionable now, and many people do not want to inquire into the consequences of their giving. Yet if we want to diminish suffering in the future, we must audit the results of our giving. It was not enough when we gave 50 million dollars for the worldwide telethon called "Live Aid" held on 13 July 1985. We should also ask two questions: 1) What happens to the donations? and 2) What are the effects of the gifts that reach their target?

The press has become very effective in answering the first question. We have learned (not to our surprise) that crash programs governed by a crisis mentality inevitably produce waste. Rats destroy stores of grain; food piled on uncovered docks is ruined by fungi; military forces steal grain that was intended for starving peasants; lack of transportation results in a sort of evaporation of food stores; and political graft increases the costs of distribution. What percentage of the donations fails to reach the targeted population? We don't know, but we are reasonably sure that the wastage is at least 30 percent and perhaps even more.

Uncovering scandalous waste is the bread and butter of reporters, but let us not be distracted by their findings, important as they are. Naturally, we want to minimize waste. But it is the second question on our list that is the more important. What do donations *that are not wasted* do to the target populations?

To answer this we must take a total ecological view of the situation. What are the shortages from which Ethiopians suffer most? The principal shortages are four: food, cropland, pasture land and forest land. Standard economics calls the first category a "product." Conventional charity concentrates on supplying this product, in order to maximize the short-run saving of lives. But all four categories are in short supply in Ethiopia. If we never go beyond supplying the first, the "product," we ultimately make dependents of the recipients. That is not good for them, or for us.

Economists call the other three categories "production factors." It is the operation of these that determines what ecologists call the "carrying capacity" of the land. Crop lands produce human food directly. Pasture lands produce food indirectly, through the intermediation of grazing animals which convert plants that are unsuitable as human food into meat which is. The role of forest lands is still more indirect, but no less important. Wood from forests is used as fuel to cook food; without cooking, grains are only minimally suitable as human food. Living forests produce a spongy mat of organic material on the surface of the ground, thus protecting slopes against loss of soil. This organic sponge also stores rainwater, releasing it gradually so that more of it is useable for agriculture and less of it does damage by creating floods and filling reservoirs with silt.

All three production factors are over-strained in Ethiopia: the population has grown beyond the present carrying capacity of the land. This is a most serious matter, because overpopulation violates the First Law of the Ecological Decalogue: *Thou shalt not transgress the carrying capacity.*

Even if the Ethiopian population never rises above its present level of 36 million, which is most unlikely, suffering will increase. Since the carrying capacity has already been transgressed, the three principal production factors, already degraded, will be degraded more as the years go by.

Now for the hard question, the question we don't want to hear asked. What do gifts of food-only do to the production factors in a population that has already grown beyond the carrying capacity of these factors? Plainly, merely maintaining the present population will make the situation of next year's population more desperate. But if gifts of food to Ethiopia enable the population to increase by another three-quarters of a million people, next year's population will be even worse off than the present one

In passing, it should be pointed out that all such statements implicitly carry a qualifying addendum: "other things being equal." It is possible that next year's weather may be unusually good, enabling the people to produce enough food locally. It is also possible that next year's weather may be worse. New political troubles or new diseases may surface next year. Since we cannot successfully predict the future, policy must be based on the "other things being equal" assumption.

We are approaching a point in population theory that is subtle and often missed. The analysis just given treats the population of a country as the operative unit. From that point of view it certainly seems irrational for a population that has already transgressed the carrying capacity to continue to increase, thus further eroding the factors of production.But the entire population of a nation is *not the operating unit* in reproduction. The operating unit is, (assuming monogamy) each marital couple, and the decision to breed or not to breed is made by a multitude of these operating units, not by the nation as a whole. Therefore, we must ask if the poor of the world are irrational in the way they breed?

It would be arrogant of us to say so. We must not forget that ready access to effective birth control is denied many poor people. Moreover, in a nation without a social security system, a large family can be a rational provision against the needs of old age. In one sense, poor people, in having many children, are acting rationally. Unfortunately, if the resources of the nation cannot be increased as fast as the population, the act which is rational for each couple—having many children—is disastrous in the end for the nation as a whole, including all the breeding couples.

Reduced to its essentials, what we call "the population problem" is a problem in how to make the rational interests of every fertile couple mesh with their rational interests as members of the larger community. The individual couple needs to be offered a pay-off for controlling the size of its family to the level indicated by national needs. Unless this fundamental problem is attacked and solved, all external food aid will, in the long run, prove futile.

Appalled at the consequences of ill-informed good intentions, it is natural that we should turn our attention to the production factors. Why not develop new genetic strains of crops that will do better in a nature-benighted land? Why not build dams to trap and conserve precious water? Why not build irrigation systems? Why not persuade the people to give up some of their cattle, which are maintained partly for prestige? Why not pay the people to replant the forests, and then build fences to protect the young trees against goats, and hire wardens to prevent desperate peasants from cutting down immature trees to get fuel to cook their food with? Why not. . . ?

Indeed, why not? Because all these measures require many years to accomplish, during which time the population continues to increase. As concerns superior genetic strains of plants, the time between a bright idea and its successful implementation is typically 20 years. In that interval, if we kept all the Ethiopians alive by external grants of food, the population would have increased by 19 million people.

Our dreams of revolutionizing tropical agriculture are flawed by one awkward fact. We dwellers of the temperate zones simply do not know much about tropical agriculture. Dams and irrigation systems require years to build; and they often increase the incidence of water-borne diseases. As for persuading a people to give up prestige-items like cattle, that is a really difficult job; and protecting developing forests against fuel-starved peasants is a task no one wants to take on. Almost all of our bright ideas for helping an overpopulated country turn out to be totally impracticable.

Once we recognize that increasing the supply of food causes an increase in the demand for food, we see that there is only one course of action that can help an overpopulated country: reducing its population. Ideally, this should be accomplished by reducing the birth rate to below the normal death rate; but, however it is done, reducing the size of the population, and then reducing the demand on the resources, is the only realistic answer to a poor country's problems. This is something outsiders cannot do; the people must do it themselves.

Certainly, this is not an easy task. China is trying to do it now, and is having some success. We should also note that China is doing the job herself; outsiders are not, *and should not be,* the principal moving agents. Outsiders may, if they wish, point out what needs to be done, though they will not be thanked for their advice. If they have the courage to repeat it often enough, the advice may finally be taken. And of course outsiders should always stand ready to furnish materials, such as contraceptives, when asked to do so.

The future, though bleak, is not hopeless—if, that is, we have the courage to base foreign aid policy on hard truths known to wise men and women at least since the time of *Ecclesiastes.* These hard truths can be expressed very simply. Every bit of food given to a hungry population that has grown beyond the carrying capacity of its environment, adversely affects the production factors and delays the day when self–reliance will be achieved. Gifts of food–only to such countries are well meant, but if we ultimately want the consequences of our actions to be good, we must refrain from making such gifts. At the same time, we must try to help needy countries understand that the so–called hunger problem is really a population problem. In the final analysis, population problem is one of making the preservation of the carrying capacity of the land the paramount concern of policy.

Garrett Hardin, Professor Emeritus of Human Ecology at the University of California at Santa Barbara, is the author of over 200 scholarly articles and monographs. Dr. Hardin's best known work is, "The Tragedy of the Commons," a broad inter–disciplinary view of international affairs which has been included in anthologies representing a wide variety of disciplines. This was followed by the essay, "Living on a Lifeboat," which further clarified his views. His most recent book, published in July, 1985 is *Filters Against Folly: How to Survive Despite Economists, Ecologists and the Merely Eloquent.*

# TOWARD A POLITICS OF HOPE:
# LESSONS FROM A HUNGRY WORLD

## Frances Moore Lappé

## Introduction:

When I began this work, now close to 15 years ago, I recall the bewildered looks of my friends. Why would anyone **choose** to spend all day, everyday, thinking about the most depressing subject in the world—hunger? What they failed to grasp, and what I want to share with you, is that rather than simply a depressing subject to be avoided, world hunger can become a powerful tool for making sense out of our increasingly complex world. World hunger, I learned, is a direct path to discovering where our own legitimate interests lie—for they lie in common with the hungry.

## Hunger: What is it?

Today's headlines cry out the news—famine, now threatening 30 million people in Africa. Already hundreds of thousands have died. This is hunger in its acute form.

But there is another form. It is less visible. It is the chronic day by day hunger in which half a billion to as many as 800 million people live. While chronic hunger rarely makes the evening news it is just as deadly. Each year it kills as many as 18 million people—more than *twice* as many as died annually during World War II.

These statistics are staggering. They shock and alarm, but several years ago I began to doubt the usefulness of such numbers. Numbers can numb, distancing us from what is actually very close to us.

So I asked myself—what really *IS hunger? Is it the gnawing pain in the stomach when we try to stay on that new diet? Is it the physical depletion that comes with chronic undernutrition? Yes, but it is more, and I became convinced that as long as we conceive of hunger only in physical measures*, we will never truly understand it, certainly not its roots.

What, I asked myself, would it mean to think of hunger in terms of *universal human feelings*, feelings that each one of us has experienced at some time in our lives? I'll mention only four such emotions, to give you an idea of what I mean.

To begin with, being hungry means making choices that no human being should ever have to make. In Guatemala today, many poor Indian families send a son to join the army. Yes, many know that this same army is responsible for killing tens of thousands of civilians, mostly the Indians themselves. But the $25 a month the army pays each soldier's family—half the total income of a typical poor family in Guatemala—may be the only means the family has to keep the rest of the children alive.

Dr. Charles Clements, a former airforce pilot and Vietnam veteran, who spent a year treating peasants in El Salvador, writes in *Witness to War* of a family he treated there whose son and daughter had died from fever and diarrhea. "Both had been lost," he writes, "in the years when Camila and her husband had chosen to pay their mortgage, a sum equal to half the value of their crop, rather than keep the money to feed their children. Each year, the choice was always the same, if they paid, their children's lives were endangered. If they didn't their land could be repossessed." Being hungry thus means *anguish*. The anguish of making impossible choices. But it is more.

In Nicaragua two years ago, I met Amanda Espinoza who until then has never had enough to feed her family. She told me that she had endured five stillbirths and watched six of her children die before the age of one. To her, being hungry means watching people you love die. It is *grief*.

Third, in this country and throughout the world, the poor are made to blame themselves for their poverty. Walking into a home in the rural Philippines, the first words I heard were an apology for the poverty of the dwelling. Thus, being hungry also means living in *humiliation*.

*Anguish, grief* and *humilation* are a part of what hunger means. But increasingly throughout the world, hunger has a fourth dimension.

In Guatemala, in 1978, I met two highland peasants. With the help of a U.S.-based voluntary aid group, they were teaching other poor peasants to make "contour ditches," reducing the erosion on the steep slopes to which they had been pushed by wealthy landowners in the valley. Two years later, the friend who had introduced us visited our Institute in San Francisco. I learned that one of the peasants I had met had been forced underground. The other had been killed. Their crime was teaching their neighbors better farming techniques; for any change that might make the poor less dependent on low-paying jobs on plantations threatens Guatemala's oligarchy. Increasingly, then, the fourth dimension of hunger is *fear*.

What if we were to refuse simply to count the hungry? What if instead we tried to understand hunger as four universal emotions—

anguish, grief, humiliation, and fear? We would discover, I believe, that how we understand hunger determines what we think are its solutions.

If we think of hunger as numbers, numbers of people with too few calories, the situation also appears to us in numbers—numbers of tons of food aid, or numbers of dollars in economic assistance. But once we begin to understand hunger as real families coping with the most painful of human emotions, we can perceive its roots: We need only ask ourselves when we have experienced any of these emotions ourselves. Hasn't it been when we have felt out of control of our lives? Powerless to protect ourselves and those we love? Hunger has thus become for me the ultimate symbol of powerlessness. ·

## The Causes of Powerlessness:

I want to pull back the layers of misunderstanding that hide the roots of hunger. So the first step is to ask: What are the **causes** of this powerlessness that lies at the very root of hunger?

Certainly it is not powerlessness before nature's scarcity! Not when the world is awash with grain. Reserves are at record highs. Not when the world produces five pounds of food every day for every woman, man and child alive. Not when a mere two percent of the world's grain output would eliminate the food deficit of all the world's 800 million hungry people. No, we cannot blame nature—not even in Africa. Even there, experts tell us that the continent could well be food self–sufficient.

Not even in Bangladesh, where 90 million people live in an area the size of Wisconsin. Even there, despite widespread hunger, many studies show that the rich alluvial soils, the ample water, and the year–round growing season of Bangladesh could not only produce enough for local self–sufficiency, Bangladesh could be a major food exporter.

Neither can we blame natural disasters, droughts and floods. Between the 1960s and the 1970s, deaths from so–called natural disaster leapt six-fold, but climatologists tell us that no weather changes can account for this drastic increase. Instead, increased deaths from drought and flood reflect a social breakdown in the structures protecting people from nature's vagaries.

If it is not people's powerlessness before nature's scarcity and her unpredictability, then what *is the cause of growing hunger?* On one level we can answer that the root lies not in a scarcity of food or land but in a scarcity of democracy. I mean by this the increasing concentration of decision–making power over all that it takes to grow and distribute food at the village level, the national level, and at the level of international commerce and finance.

First, at the village level, fewer and fewer people control more and more land. A United Nations study of 83 countries showed that less than five percent of the rural landholders control three-quarters of the land. For example, in El Salvador, by the mid-seventies, a mere six families had come to control as much land as 300,000 small peasant producers.

With fewer families controlling an ever greater share, more and more people have no land at all. Since 1960, the number of landless in Central America has multiplied fourfold. By the mid-seventies, in twenty third world countries, 50 percent or more of the rural people were effectively landless, deprived of the most basic resource needed to feed their families.

The village level is but one level of concentrating power. There is a second, the concentration of decision-making in the hands of national governments unaccountable to their people. They answer only to a small elite, lavishing credit and other help on them, and on a military force to protect their privileges. In the third world, expenditures on arms leapt fourfold in the decade ending in 1980. In Ethiopia the government is today spending more on its military than on all other budget categories combined. Such governments actively, and with increasing brutality, resist genuine reforms which would make fairer the distribution of control over food resources.

Such governments love terms like "land reform," but we needn't be deceived. In El Salvador, the U.S. AID designed reform left untouched the most powerful—the big coffee estates—and the most powerless, the 60 percent or more of rural people with no land at all. By selling, on time, small plots to tenant farmers, all the "reform" did accomplish was to lock into perpetual debt poor families on plots too infertile and small to support them. Similarly, in the Philippines, Ferdinand Marcos declared land reform almost as soon as he took office in 1972. But under this one—family rule, land ownership in the Philippines has become more concentrated, not less, and the Philippine people are among the hungriest in all Asia, according to the World Health Organization.

Thus, the second level on which we can document the increasing concentration of decision-making at the root of hunger is at the level of national governments beholden to narrow elites.

But there is yet a third level—that of international commerce and finance. A handful of corporations dominate world trade in most of the raw commodities which are the lifeblood of third world economies. According to the U.N., of the approximately $200 billion that consumers in the industrial countries pay for agricultural products from the third world, only 15 percent returns to the third world countries, and of course only a fraction of that to the producers themselves.

Dependent on international markets over which they have no control, third world producing countries have seen the prices of every single one of their commodities—with the sole exception of cocoa—fall in real terms in the last 30 years.One example sums up the drastic consequences of this price deterioration: Any gain that Africa might have seen from billions in foreign aid since the 1970's has been entirely wiped out by losses in revenue from declining prices for its exports.

So far, however, we have only removed one layer of misunderstanding in our effort to uncover the roots of hunger. We have identified the problem not in the scarcity of resources, but in the scarcity of democracy, reflected in the tightening control over economic resources.But, we must dig deeper. We must ask why. *Why have we allowed this to happen, even at the cost of millions of needless deaths each year?*

Why do we rationalize and condone, and indeed shore up with our tax dollars, systems that generate such needless suffering? Even here in our own country, where, according to a recent Harvard physicians' study, one in ten of us is so poor we are at risk of hunger?

### Is Our Powerlessness Self-imposed by Economic Dogma?

Peeling off another layer, I've concluded that at the root of hunger lies our own self–imposed powerlessness before economic dogma.

Eighteenth century intellectual advances forced us to relinquish our ever-so-comforting notion of an interventionist God who would put the human house aright. We faced a frightening void and we have desperately sought a substitute concept—something, *anything* to relieve us of the responsibility of moral reasoning. With Newton's discovery of laws governing the physical world and with Darwin's discovery of laws governing nature, we seized upon the notion of parallel laws governing the social world, laws that we could place above human intervention.These absolutes I call our false gods, precisely because, though they be human inventions, we have made them sacred. Placing ourselves at the mercy of dogma, we acquiesce to hunger. This is the tragedy.

### The Market

There are two major tenets of the economic dogma now ruling the West: the market and property rights. We must consider the consequences of making them absolute, rather than simply devices to serve our values.

First is the market. We certainly hear a lot about the free market's virtues these days. And who can deny that it *is* a handy device for distributing goods? Any society which has tried to do away with it has faced some mighty serious headaches.The problem arises in converting a useful device into an absolute. We become blind to its pitfalls.

What are the central pitfalls of the market that directly relate to the causes of hunger? I recently had the dubious pleasure of debating Milton Friedman. Now, Nobel Laureate Friedman insists that the greatest virtue of the free market is that it responds to individual preferences. "But wait," I said to Dr. Friedman. "I thought that the preference of most individuals is to eat when we are hungry. Yet more than half a billion people living in market economies are *not* eating." The lesson is unmistakable: *the market doesn't respond to individual preferences, it responds to money.*

Nowhere is this obvious truth clearer than in the flow of food in world trade: While we think of the third world as dependent on imports, actually we in the industrial countries are the largest importers of agricultural commodities, importing almost 70 percent of all farm commodities traded. The U.S., known for our cowboys and 16-ounce steaks, is actually the largest importer of beef in the world. This flow from the hungry to the overfed is simply the market at work. Exports from hunger intensify even as hunger deepens. Why does this happen?

As the third world poor are increasingly pushed from the land and must compete for jobs as day-laborers, they are less and less able to make their demand for food register in the market. With a stagnant or shrinking domestic market for basic foods, naturally those who remain in control of the land orient their production to the highest-paying consumers, and they are abroad. Thus, we have a Global Supermarket in which even the Fido and Felix in North America can outbid the hungry in the third world.

My first sight of the Global Supermarket occurred when driving in northwest Mexico in the late 1970's. I wound through land made productive with expensive irrigation systems, paid for with billions of pesos from the Mexican government, supposedly to grow food for hungry Mexican peasants. But I didn't see corn or beans growing. No, I saw mile after mile of cotton, and then tomatoes, cucumbers and peppers—all destined for North America!

Stopping at a government agricultural research station, I asked: Why are these farmers growing tomatoes and specialty vegetables for North American tables when Mexicans are going hungry? The agronomist sat down and scratched out a few numbers. "It's quite simple," he said. "An entrepreneur here can make 20 times more growing tomatoes for export than growing the basic foods of our people."

Several years later, I recall landing in the rural Philippines. From my airplane window as far as the eye could see were banana trees. Only a few years earlier that land had grown a variety of crops, many for local consumption. Then transnational firms, including Del Monte and Dole, offered contracts to the biggest local landowners to produce bananas for the lucrative Japanese market. It wasn't difficult to push the peasants from the land. After all, in the third world, who has a legal title to land?

And what poor peasant could afford a lawyer's defense? So within 10 years, 50,000 acres were taken over by banana growers.

Since 1970, while hunger deepens, export crop production throughout the world has grown two–and–a–half times faster than the production of basic foods.In my view, however, the most dramatically telling consequence of the market's distribution within a world of gross inequalities is the disposition of the world's grain supply. When I wrote *Diet for a Small Planet* in 1971, I learned that about one-third of the world's grain was going to feed livestock. I was shocked. But when I returned to do the research for the tenth anniversary edition of that book, I learned that fully *one–half* of the world's grain is now going to feed livestock. Even in famine–stricken Africa, the demand for feed (that is the demand that the market can register) is growing twice as fast as the demand for food.

The growth of the Global Supermarket is a reflection of the problem, not the problem itself. It reflects the increasing gap between rich and poor, between those few who can live by their wealth, and those many unable to live by their work.The lesson to be learned is that left to its own devices, the market simply reflects and reinforces the deadly wealth gap in our world. Thus it must be seen for what it is, a useful device, and nothing more. We must no longer delude ourselves into thinking that it registers the needs and wishes of real people; it measures the power of wealth.

The second pitfall of the market is that it is blind, and therefore misleads us. It is *blind* to the human and resource costs of the productive impetus it claims to foster.

Let's return to an example close to home. Over the 1970's, our agricultural exports boomed, growing sixfold in value in only a decade. In one year our agricultural exports brought in over $40 billion in foreign exchange. In terms of the market, this was viewed as a bonanza. All that grain could pay for imported oil.

But what did the market fail to tell us? The market couldn't tell us that just producing all that grain required an energy expenditure equivalent to at least one-third of what we earn by exporting it. Furthermore, the market couldn't tell us about the topsoil eroded from prime farmland at an accelerated rate, up by 39 percent in just the first three years of the export boom. Nor could the market tell us that the push to export means that groundwater is being pumped from the earth much faster than nature can replenish it.

Neither did, neither could, the market inform us of the social cost of all–out production—of the tens of thousands of good farmers pushed from the land and hundreds of rural communities destroyed. In theory, the market rewards hard work and production. But that is theory. In reality, the market forces hard work and production. But it only rewards those who can expand. And who are they? Just as in the third world, they are those with considerable equity so that they have access to credit. They can therefore expand to make up in volume what they are losing in profits per acre, as the production push leads to price–depressing gluts.

To the social cost of the devastation of livelihoods, of increased rural landlessness, and of the shocking phenomenon of whole rural communities and farmers on food stamps—to all this the market is blind.

But the market, left to its own devices, has a third fatal drawback, undermining deeply held values. It leads to the concentration of economic power, concentration that directly contributes to hunger and makes genuine political democracy impossible. This is relatively easy to see when we look at the third world. The connection between hunger in El Salvador and six families controlling as much land as 300,000 peasants is obvious. Yet why can't we see the connection at home between the growing concentration of economic power and needless human suffering?

Cast more fully at the mercy of the vagaries of international markets in the 1970's, American farming experienced perhaps the most dramatic concentration of reward in our history. In just one decade the top one percent of farmers by sales, increased their share of net farm income from 16 percent to 60 percent. Yet there is no evidence that the greater efficiency of this top one percent justifies such an extreme concentration of reward. Mid–sized family farms, many of which are in jeopardy of losing their land, capture virtually all economies of scale in farming.

This third pitfall of the market, its tendency toward the concentration of economic power beyond anything efficiency justifies, draws our attention to the fourth and final point I want to make about the market as dogma. Clinging with blind faith to the ideology of the market, as price setter and as allocator of resources, hides the truth that nowhere are markets *free*. While ideologues view the market as the interplay of impersonal, automatic forces, in fact, because all markets lead to concentration, all markets reflect the disproportionate power of a relatively few actors. Nowhere is this truer than in world agricultural trade, as we have seen.

Now, facing unflinchingly the pitfalls of the market does not mean that we throw out the market dogma in favor of another dogma such as top–down state planning. Rather it means that we approach the market as a useful device, and nothing more. We ask ourselves: *under what circumstances can the market serve our values?* Then we work to ensure those conditions.

Under what conditions therefore could market distribution serve to reduce hunger? Under what conditions could the market respond to human preferences as Milton Friedman would have it? Consider the simple proposition that *the more widely dispersed is purchasing power, the more the market will respond to actual human preferences.*

As we have already seen, the opposite is true. That is, where income is highly skewed, the preferences of the majority are ignored by the market—whether it be bananas flowing from hunger in the Philippines to Japan or beef shipped from hunger in Central America to our tables.

But what can we say in a **positive** vein? Is there evidence of relative equality of income allowing the market to work to eliminate hunger? We can say that those very few market economies in the world that have successfully eliminated hunger enjoy a more even distribution of income than we do here, the Scandanavian countries, for example. In the third world we also have some instructive examples. Taiwan has much less hunger than, for example, the Dominican Republic. While both are market economies, Taiwan implemented a widespread land reform in the 1950's and laid the basis for somewhat more equal access to resources. We can also compare the Indian state of Kerala with other states in India. The death rate of babies in Kerala (a good nutrition measure) is half the all–India average, in part because land reform and a strong union movement there resulted in a wider distribution of economic power.

So, if we truly believe in the value of the market in enhancing human freedom, our goal should be clear: to work for all policies that reduce rather than reinforce the concentration of income and wealth.

But how *within a market system*, and *only* within a market system in which everything (land, food, human skills, etc.) is bought and sold with no restriction, can we work toward a more equal distribution of buying power? The answer is *we cannot*. For the historical record shows that the market leads in the opposite direction—toward concentration. In other words, the market, left to its own devices, *undermines the very condition so obviously necessary for it to serve human needs.*

But, if we agree that tossing out the market would be foolish, and yet we want to let go of rigid dogma and take our rightful responsibility as moral agents, what do we do?Unfortunately, to answer this question, we must face the second major stumbling block posed by our economic dogma, the absolute notion of unlimited private control of productive property. The dogma of property rights allows us to swallow as fair and inevitable the accelerating consolidation of our own farmland in fewer hands, and in absentee ownership, just as we have long seen in the third world. Today in Iowa, the very symbol of family farm America, half or more of the land is now rented, not owner–operated. Similarly, we accept the accelerating concentration of corporate power; today one–tenth of one percent of U.S. corporations control two–thirds of corporate assets.

Believing that our very nation was built on the right to unlimited private control of productive property, many Americans view this right as the most basic protector of our freedom. But Yale economic philosopher Charles Lindblom points out what we often overlook. Very concisely he has written, "Income producing property is the bulwark of liberty only for those who have it!" I must add to that most Americans don't have it. Eighty percent of Americans own no stock at all. Not only do most of us have no income-producing property, the majority of Americans have no net savings.

Now, while President Reagan and many other Americans may believe that the right to unlimited private control of productive property is the essence of the American Way, this was certainly not the vision of our founders. It was not their understanding of property. In the eyes of our founders, property rights were not absolute but were linked to the concept of the common good. Dismayed over the misery caused by land concentration in Europe, Thomas Jefferson wrote to James Madison in 1785, "...legislators cannot invent too many devices for subdividing property." Indeed, Jefferson wanted to redistribute land every generation.

In their view, property could only serve liberty when it is widely dispersed. The right to property was valid only when it served a useful function in society, that is, when it did not interfere with all people's need to own property. Benjamin Franklin, for example, argued that society had the right to reclaim "superfluous property" and use it as deemed best for the common good.

Thus, central to my concept of a "politics of hope", one breaking free from constraints of dogma, is a fundamental re-thinking of the meaning of ownership, certainly ownership of resources on which all humanity depends. We see a worldwide movement toward such re-thinking already underway. In this re-thinking, ownership of productive resources, instead of an absolute to be placed above other values, becomes *a cluster of rights and responsibilities in the service of our values.* It is neither the rigid capitalist concept of private ownership nor the rigid statist concept of public ownership.

Where do I see movement toward such re-thinking? In 1982 I visited one of the most productive industrial complexes in Europe. In Mondragon, in the Basque region of Spain, 90 or so enterprises integrated within their own banking system, are a technical training school and social services which are entirely owned and governed by the workers themselves. This noncapitalist, nonstatist form of ownership results in very different priorities and another set of values. During, for example, the recession of the early 1980's when Spain suffered 15 percent unemployment, virtually no one in Mondragon was laid off. Worker-owners were retrained to meet the needs of the changing economy.

We can also detect a values-first approach to ownership in the third world. Since 1979, the Institute for Food and Development Policy has served as an unpaid adviser to the Nicaraguan agrarian reform. Nicaragua's flexible, nondogmatic approach to reform has impressed us most. The keystone of the agrarian reform is not the elimination of private property; indeed many more landowners have been generated by the reform. The keystone is attaching an obligation to the right to ownership.

If you know anything about Latin America, you are undoubtedly aware that historically the large land owners, who control the best land, have left most of it unplanted, preferring to graze cattle or simply let it sit. A study of Central America in the 1970s showed that only 14 percent of the land held by the biggest landowners was actually planted. So the theme of the Nicaraguan reform is simple: "Idle lands to working hands."

If you are directly working your land, not renting it out, and you are making it produce, there is no ceiling to the amount of land you can own (in contrast to so many reforms that have tried to enforce a rigid limit). If you are not making the land produce, you will have it taken away and given to those who have gone hungry for want of land. The land is given free of charge, also in contrast to so many other so called reforms leaving peasants as indebted after the reform as they were before. The concept of ownership is thus protected, but not above the higher value of life itself, the right of all human beings to eat.

Do these examples sound far away, irrevelant, even alien to our own experience? Closer to home, consider the recent decision of Nebraskans on this very question of farmland ownership. A few years ago they passed an amendment to their state's consititution which said, in effect, you have to be a farmer to own farmland. Corporations like Prudential Insurance which had been buying up Nebraska farmland could buy no more. In their overwhelming support for this amendment, Nebraskans put the value of dispersed ownership, in family farm agriculture, above the absolute notion of anyone's right to buy whatever their dollars can pay for. They certainly didn't end private ownership, but they attached an obligation to it—the obligation to protect the higher, social value of family farm agriculture itself.

I introduced my comments on property rights in response to the question: what would be required to achieve such a dispersion of economic power that the market could actually reflect human needs rather than the demands of wealth? Part of the answer, I have suggested, lies in rethinking property rights as a device to serve higher values, not an end in themselves. But there is an additional approach worthy of consideration.

Given that the movement toward more fair distribution of buying power requires time, and given that even under the best of circumstances, the market by its nature has its ups and downs, many civilized people have simply decided that *that which is necessary to life itself* should not be left to the vagaries of the market.

So in Kerala India, one–third of the grain is distributed through publically controlled fair–price shops. And in that state, despite low per capita food production, infant morality is half the all–India average, as mentioned previously.

In Sweden, to avoid good farmers going under due to the vagaries of markets, Swedes have simply said that family farm agriculture is too precious to be left to the market. Wholesale food prices are therefore set by negotiation, not the market. Periodically, representatives of the government, food companies, retail food cooperatives and farmers themselves sit down at the bargaining table. Retail food prices, however, are determined by the market. (Contrast the experience of American farmers who don't know from one day to the next what price their commodities will bring!) Moreover, we should not overlook the fact that all western idustrialized countries, with the exception of the United States, have concluded that health care is too important to life itself to be left to the market.

I present these examples, hardly as the final word. I present them as signs of growing courage to confront the rigid "ism's" into which we have trapped ourselves. This is true courage to put our deepest values first and judge economic policies according to how they serve those values, rather than the other way around.

I have been attempting to peel away the layers of cause and misunderstanding that surround world hunger. At the surface layer, we can identify the root of hunger in powerlessness imposed by the increasing concentration of decision-making power over all that it takes to grow and distribute food. But on a deeper level, I believe that the root of hunger lies in our self-imposed powerlessness before the economic rules that, if taken dogmatically, create that concentration of power to begin with! It is thus this rule of dogma that must be challenged, if we are to end hunger.

### The Impact of Our Dogma on the Hungry Abroad

But this rule of dogma—the war of the giant "ism's" capitalism versus statism—has perhaps its most devastating impact on the hungry through the way in which it directs our country's foreign policy. Viewing the world divided between two competing "ism's" our government becomes blind to hunger. Worse, it willingly abets the very concentration of power at its roots.

Thus, our foreign aid becomes, not a channel through which we can put ourselves on the side of hungry people, but a weapon our government uses to make the world conform to its dogma. As a result, the direction of our foreign aid has nothing to do with need. High-income recipients of U.S. foreign aid get almost 12 dollars per capita, but in the low-income countries, it is fifty cents per person, a 23 fold difference. Today Central America receives per capita *six times* more food aid than Sub-Saharan Africa, despite terrible famine there.

Military aid and general budgetary support to allies has grown in recent years from about half to almost three-fourths of our foreign aid. Militarization is dramatic: over the last five years, the number of African countries receiving U.S. military assistance has leapt from 16 to 37. While

food aid to Africa has fallen, military assistance in the prop
allocations to that continent has shot up three-fold compared to

The role of U.S. foreign aid, lavished on anti-democratic r ⌟....cs in countries like El Salvador (which follows Israel as the second biggest per capita recipient), the Philippines and Pakistan is not to reduce poverty but to shore up governments. No matter how brutally these countries deny basic human rights and as long as they at least claim to be on "our" side in the context of economic ideology, they continue to receive aid. Under the Reagan administration, our foreign aid is now also *explicitly* conditioned on recipient countries removing any restrictions on the market and promoting exports. "Free enterprise development" has replaced "basic needs" as the favored rhetoric of aid officials.

But if not through foreign aid, what is our responsibility to the hungry? To answer means first that we admit the tragic failures in meeting human needs of *both* capitalism as we know it and statism as we fear it. Can this failure be denied when deaths from hunger equal the toll of a Hiroshima bomb every three days? Second, this implies accepting the need for fundamental change. Finally, we must understand that pressure for such change is inevitable. We do not have to create it. People do not go on watching their children die of hunger needlessly. At first they protest peaceably, for no one risks their lives if they can avoid it. But if their peaceful demands are met with violence, they will risk their lives. I recall a Central American peasant telling me why he had ultimately taken up arms: "For years I watched the owner of the plantation call in a doctor to treat his sick dogs, while my own children, weakened by hunger, died of simple childhood diseases."

Since pressure for change is inevitable, we have a choice. We can attempt to block changes, shoring up governments which stand in the way of the hungry or, if we truly understand the roots of hunger, we can get out of the way, remove the obstacles, and give change a chance.

Now, many Americans might agree, I hope, with much of what I have said but when faced with the implications they often stop and say, "but, but, but. . . we can't do that! If we remove our support and 'give change a chance' the Soviet Union will fill in the void, imposing their own version of economic dogma. Nothing new will be allowed to emerge, only another Cuba." I have thought about this fear long and hard. I understand it. But let us look again at just what choices we have.

On the one hand we can let our government continue on its present course but where will this lead? One country has come for me to symbolize the horror at the end of that course, it is Guatemala. There we have consistently blocked change; our military and economic aid since the 1950's has abetted the overthrow of a democratic government and has strengthened the hand of the elite-controlled government that has murdered tens of thousands of Indians, all opposition leaders (even moderate

Christian democrats) and hundreds of churchpeople. Guatemala has the worst human rights record in Latin America. Poor Guatemalans are today living in a state of seige; Guatemala is a "nation of prisoners," according to Amnesty International.Guatemala represents one choice and I have rejected that choice.

Or, as I have said, we can give change a chance. Primarily this would mean simply forcing our government to obey the law—both U.S. laws and the international treaties that forbid much of our government's current policy of shoring up repressive governments and attempting to overthrow those like Nicaragua which do not fit our dogma.I think there are two possible outcomes.

Yes, one outcome could be the emergence of another Cuba. But then we have to ask, what harm has been caused us by Cuba? I could make the case that it has been more of a drain on our adversary, the Soviet Union, than a threat to us. Indeed if we had been trading with Cuba as we now are with China, Cuba's development would have been a boon to our economy.

However, I believe that, there is another possibility. Studying underdevelopment all of these years, one thing of which I am certain is that every country emerging from decades, even centuries, of domination by an elite beholden to outsiders will, above all else,want to chart its *own* path. Such peoples will want to do it their way! The last thing on earth they want is to become a puppet of another superpower.

My close–up observation of Nicaragua during the last six years has strongly confirmed my hunch that this demand to chart their own unique course is the most likely outcome of giving change a chance. Determined not to be a satellite of the Soviet Union, yet knowing that it needed support from abroad, Nicaragua has worked for what it calls "mixed dependency." At least until very recently, only 20 percent of its aid and trade have been with the Soviet bloc. Eighty percent of agriculture and 60 percent of the economy as a whole are in private hands.

Perhaps Nicaragua's most dramatic break with past revolutions was one of the first acts of the interim Sandinista government that took over when Somoza fled. It abolished the death penalty, and it gave every captured National Guardsman the benefit of a trial. Thus, if we can escape the spell cast by Washington, we can view Nicaragua as an example, not of a new model of development, but a lesson in the possibility of real change. Just because something is not like us, it does not have to be our enemy. Emerging peoples *do* want to break free of *both* rigid dogmas—capitalism and statism.

Appreciating this truth is asking a lot of us, I know, but not more than we should be capable of. Appreciation of all people on earth, this attitude of openness to the possibility of something *new* should be our very birthright. Remember that when our nation was born, its very principles were considered madness! Of the Declaration of Independence, a high-ranking British office wrote, "A more false and atrocious document was never fabricated by the hands of man." Near his death, James Madison said of our new born nation that America has proved what before was believed to be impossible. Shouldn't we thus be willing to give change a chance in the Third World?

## Conclusions

Now you may think that I have come a long way from hunger and its roots, but I have not. I believe that the causes of hunger are rooted in belief systems that rob us of our power, that teach us to abdicate before the false gods of economic dogma both our moral responsibility and our innate human sympathies for each other's well-being.

I have challenged us to break loose. This is a risk, but there is no change without risk. We must risk challenging deeply ingrained ways of thinking, for only if we can experience ourselves changing, will we believe the world can change. Willing to change ourselves, we are ready to understand a "politics of hope," not blind faith in models, but honest hope gleaned from looking at real examples of human courage and innovation from Nebraska to Nicaragua, from Spain to India.

My father just turned 70 not too long ago. He is a very thoughtful man. One day he found himself mulling over the fact that if you just multiply his age by 100, you have pretty much the history of civilization as we know it. I was taken aback. I tend to think of human civilization as being so old that surely we should have given up our folly by now. But if my father's lifetime represents only one-hundredth of our history, maybe we are just in our adolescence! Maybe our tragic stubbornness, clinging to forms that sacrifice life to human-made economic law, is just a sign of the fanaticism of youth. Maybe we are on the brink of a new confidence born of greater maturity in which we have the courage to put our values first.

We were warned against the consequences of following false-gods. But we mortals did not listen. So now we face the ultimate reward, the very survival of life on earth. Perhaps with this realization, we will be called to the higher stage of maturity now required of us.

Thus a "politics of hope" lies in our courage to unflinchingly challenge the false gods of economic dogma. A "politics of hope" lies in garnering the confidence to trust in our deepest moral sensibilities, our deepest emotional intuitions about our connectedness to others' well-being. On this basis we will be able to challenge dogma, demanding that it serve our values rather than continuing to contort our values so that dogma remains intact, while our fellow human beings starve in the midst of plenty.

Frances Moore Lappé, author and co-founder of the Institute for Food and Development Policy, is a leading spokesperson for the growing numbers of individuals and organizations concerned with world hunger. Among her many publications, *Diet For a Small Planet* is a classic which has sold over two million copies and been translated into five different languages. She is currently writing a book which explores the traditional values that have molded our nation's economic life. Articles written by her have appeared in such diverse publications as *Harper's, The Nation, Chemistry, Commonweal, and the New York Times.*